Asia Bible Commentary Series

JOEL, NAHUM, AND MALACHI

ASIA THEOLOGICAL ASSOCIATION

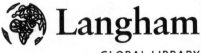

Langham

GLOBAL LIBRARY

Asia Bible Commentary Series

JOEL, NAHUM, AND MALACHI

Joseph Too Shao and Rosa Ching Shao

General Editor
Andrew B. Spurgeon

Old Testament Consulting Editors
Yohanna Katanacho, Joseph Shao, Havilah Dharamraj

New Testament Consulting Editors
Steve Chang, Brian Wintle

© 2021 Joseph Too Shao and Rosa Ching Shao

Published 2021 by Langham Global Library
An imprint of Langham Publishing
www.langhampublishing.org

Langham Publishing and its imprints are a ministry of Langham Partnership

Langham Partnership
PO Box 296, Carlisle, Cumbria, CA3 9WZ, UK
www.langham.org

Published in partnership with Asia Theological Association

ATA
QCC PO Box 1454–1154, Manila, Philippines
www.ataasia.com

ISBNs:
978-1-83973-265-2 Print
978-1-83973-523-3 ePub
978-1-83973-524-0 Mobi
978-1-83973-525-7 PDF

British Library Cataloguing-in-Publication Data
A catalogue record for this book is available from the British Library

ISBN: 978-1-83973-265-2

Cover & Book Design: projectluz.com

To

Billie Hanks Jr. and Carol Anne

whose mentorship in disciple-making
has called us back into fulfilling Christ's Great Commission
for such a time as this –
inspiring our vision,
igniting our passion,
and impacting our lives and the lives of those who follow us;

Andrew and Grace Liuson

whose friendship with us spans over three Shao generations –
encouraging us in times of need,
empowering us in times of plenty,
and enabling us to keep our eyes fixed on Jesus,
the Author and Perfecter of our faith.

CONTENTS

Commentary

Topics

SERIES PREFACE

What's unique about the *Asia Bible Commentary Series*? It is a commentary series written especially for Asian Christians, which incorporates and addresses Asian concerns, cultures, and practices. As Asian scholars – either by nationality, passion, or calling – the authors identify with the biblical text, understand it culturally, and apply its principles in Asian contexts to strengthen the churches in Asia. Missiologists tell us that Christianity has shifted from being a Western majority religion to a South, South-Eastern, and Eastern majority religion and that the church is growing at an unprecedented rate in these regions. This series meets the need for evangelical commentaries written specifically for an Asian audience.

This is not to say that Asian churches and Asian Christians don't want to partner with Western Christians and churches or that they spurn Western influences. A house divided cannot stand. The books in this series complement the existing Western commentaries by taking into consideration the cultural nuances familiar to the Eastern world so that the Eastern readership is not inundated with Western clichés and illustrations that they are unable to relate to and which may not be applicable to them.

The mission of this series is "to produce resources that are biblical, pastoral, contextual, missional, and prophetic for pastors, Christian leaders, cross-cultural workers, and students in Asia." While using approved exegetical principles, the writers strive to be culturally relevant, offer practical applications, and provide clear explanations of the texts so that readers can grow in understanding and maturity in Christ, and so that Christian leaders can guide their congregations into maturity. May we be found faithful to this endeavor and may God be glorified!

Andrew B. Spurgeon
General Editor

AUTHORS' PREFACE

In 2019, in God's perfect timing, we stepped down from our full-time positions at the Biblical Seminary of the Philippines (BSOP) after almost 40 years of theological ministry. Those years are precious to us and we reflect on them with gratitude because we learned so much as we served by preaching, teaching, writing, administrating, caring, counseling, and even giving. Nevertheless, the term *retirement* has since taken a different meaning. We say this because we are still doing all these ministerial tasks, in a wider context and in broader ways, as God continues to open doors for us beyond the gates of BSOP. So now we replace *retirement* with a better term: global *re-assignment*!

When Dr. Andrew B. Spurgeon, General Editor of the ABCS, assigned us to write this commentary on Joel, Nahum, and Malachi, we counted it a joy and a privilege. We have studied and researched these three books for many years, as we shared God's message of faith, hope, and love whenever and wherever opportunities arose. Joseph even delivered a series of lectures on the book of Malachi on Good TV for Chinese audiences worldwide.

Who would have thought that communities all over the world would be in lockdown because of the COVID-19 pandemic! Major events – from this deadly virus to the global movement for racial justice – have colored the year 2020. It was a shocking and unsettling time for people from all walks of life in all parts of the world. If we are to stand our ground amid the uncertainties that surround us, our minds and thoughts must be reset according to God's word and our hearts must return to the Lord.

In a world where technology and scientific research having reached great heights, a rapidly mutating virus caused a global pandemic that reduced all humankind to an equal level of vulnerability. Everyone is impacted. No one is immune. Anyone could be the next positive case! The book of Joel describes a locust plague that would devastate the land of Israel during postexilic times. We are warned of the coming "day of the Lord" – a day of terrible darkness and gloom. Yet, even in the midst of these frightening realities, the prophet Joel has a message of hope for God's people: "And everyone who calls on the name of the Lord will be saved" (Joel 2:32a)!

The message from the preexilic prophet Nahum predicts the destruction of Assyria, the archenemy of Israel and Judah. The book contains vivid and dramatic descriptions of the battle scenes leading to the overthrow of this seemingly invincible foe. Thus, Nahum's pronouncement is a comfort, consolation, and cheer to the people of God: "Look, there on the mountains, the feet of one who brings good news, who proclaims peace!" (Nah 1:15a). God does not delay to bring judgment and punishment upon the wicked Assyrians. In times of trouble, God proves himself a stronghold and refuge for those who trust him. Today, as human atrocities magnify and suffering increases in so many parts of our world, we need to trust that God is just and that he is still in control.

God's messenger, the prophet Malachi, confronts false worship and lip service among God's chosen people during the postexilic period. This is a serious time of reckoning. The people are questioning God's love and presence in their lives but they themselves – from the priests to the people – are guilty of unfaithfulness and unrighteousness. Yet, the Lord assures them of his unchanging love: "I the LORD do not change" (Mal 3:6a). The upheavals of the year 2020 challenge us to view our world through the lens of God's word and to take an inventory of how we live in this world as the children of God. Is our faith lived out authentically? Are we truly walking our talk by a commitment to holy living? Are we being faithful to God's call to be *in* the world, yet not *of* the world? Despite the many voices shouting out contrary messages, are we standing firm in faith as we await the return of the Lord? The Lord gives this assurance to all those who fear and honor him: "they will be my treasured possession. I will spare them, just as a father has compassion and spares his son who serves him" (Mal 3:17).

These three books do not come from the same time in Israel's history and these three prophets are not contemporaries. Yet, they all point us to both the imminent judgment and the incomparable love of God. The Lord reaches out to people who, despite being blessed by him, are prone to stray from him; he remains faithful and just in all his words and works, even when they are unfaithful. This is the theme that unifies these three books. These three prophets proclaim God's unchanging word in our fast-changing and challenging world. May each of these books lead each of us to a deeper faith in our Lord and Savior who *will* return! As Charles G. Finney once said, "Great sermons lead the people to praise the preacher. Good preaching leads the people to praise the Savior" (*The Memoirs of Charles G. Finney*).

Joseph and Rosa Shao
Biblical Seminary of the Philippines

ACKNOWLEDGMENTS

We thank the board, faculty, and staff of the Biblical Seminary of the Philippines for their continuous encouragement as we keep up with many writing projects. We also thank the various seminaries in Asia, Australia, New Zealand, Europe, and North America that have sharpened our skills in biblical exposition and contextual application of texts as we teach and preach in their midst.

We acknowledge Dr. David Sang-Bok Kim, the former chairman of ATA, who encouraged Joseph to serve as ATA's fourth General Secretary. This experience has helped Joseph to understand the broader context of Asia as he travels to meet the members of ATA. We truly appreciate Dr. John Walton's enduring friendship and thank him for introducing Joseph to friends at his postgraduate studies, Hebrew Union College, and for his lovely endorsement.

We thank God for his grace that has enabled us to write this commentary during this period of the COVID-19 pandemic. We have had ample time to reflect and write, and also to have fun with our three grown-up children and their spouses – Jathniel and Rissah, Ruth and Daniel, and Reuelle and Matthew – and our grandchildren – Roi Jathniel, Abigail Faith, Nicolas Wesley, and Elizabeth Rose. May all of them come to know the Lord whose steadfast love blesses us every day (Lam 3:22–23)!

LIST OF ABBREVIATIONS

BOOKS OF THE BIBLE

Old Testament

Gen, Exod, Lev, Num, Deut, Josh, Judg, Ruth, 1–2 Sam, 1–2 Kgs, 1–2 Chr, Ezra, Neh, Esth, Job, Ps/Pss, Prov, Eccl, Song, Isa, Jer, Lam, Ezek, Dan, Hos, Joel, Amos, Obad, Jonah, Mic, Nah, Hab, Zeph, Hag, Zech, Mal

New Testament

Matt, Mark, Luke, John, Acts, Rom, 1–2 Cor, Gal, Eph, Phil, Col, 1–2 Thess, 1–2 Tim, Titus, Phlm, Heb, Jas, 1–2 Pet, 1–2–3 John, Jude, Rev

BIBLE TEXTS AND VERSIONS

Divisions of the canon

NT	New Testament
OT	Old Testament

Ancient texts and versions

LXX	Septuagint
MT	Masoretic Text

Modern versions

ESV	English Standard Version
KJV	King James Version
NASB	New American Standard Bible
NIV	New International Version
NRSV	New Revised Standard Version
RSV	Revised Standard Version

Journals, reference works, and series

ABCS	Asia Bible Commentary Series
AYBC	Anchor Yale Bible Commentary

AYBD	Anchor Yale Bible Dictionary
BBR	*Bulletin for Biblical Research*
CBQ	*Catholic Biblical Quarterly*
CBR	*Currents in Biblical Research*
EBC	Expositor's Bible Commentary Revised
Int	*Interpretation*
JBL	*Journal of Biblical Literature*
JBQ	*Jewish Biblical Quarterly*
JSOT	*Journal for the Study of the Old Testament*
NBC	New Bible Commentary
NBD	New Bible Dictionary
NCBC	New Century Bible Commentary
NIBC	New International Biblical Commentary
NICOT	New International Commentary on Old Testament
NIVAC	NIV Application Commentary
OTE	Old Testament Essays
OTL	Old Testament Library
SABC	South Asia Bible Commentary
TynBul	*Tyndale Bulletin*
TOTC	Tyndale Old Testament Commentary
VT	*Vetus Testamentum*
WBC	Word Biblical Commentary
WeBC	Westminster Biblical Commentary
WEC	Wycliffe Exegetical Commentary
ZAW	*Zeitschrift für die alttestamentliche Wissenschaft*

THE BOOK OF JOEL

INTRODUCTION

AUTHORSHIP AND DATE

The name "Joel" means "The Lord (YHWH) is God" or "God is the Lord (YHWH)." The book gives no information about the prophet except to tell us that his father's name was Pethuel (1:1) – a name that is not mentioned elsewhere in the Bible.

The book makes no reference to either a date or a king. Scholars have proposed three possible dates for composition of the book: first, a ninth- to mid-eighth-century date; second, a mid-eighth-century date; and third, a postexilic date.

The traditional early dating derives from the book's position in the Hebrew canon, between Hosea and Amos. The theme of returning to the Lord (2:12–17; compare Hos 14:1; Amos 4:6, 8–11) and "the day of the LORD" (2:1; compare Amos 5:18–20) seem to fit the ongoing struggle against Baal worship. The mid-eighth-century date links the destruction of agriculture produce (1:5–7; compare Hos 2:9–13) with the locust invasion (1:2–4; compare Amos 4:9; 7:1–3).[1]

But recent scholarship favors a postexilic date for Joel. One reason for this view is its placement in the Septuagint – the Greek translation of the Old Testament – after Hosea, Amos, and Micah, which seems to imply that Joel is not necessarily associated with the eighth-century prophets. Since the internal evidence speaks of the destruction of Jerusalem (3:1–6), the argument is that Joel must have been written after 586 BC. Another argument in favor of a postexilic setting is the references to fasting at the temple (1:14–17) – which was considered an exilic and postexilic practice – and the mention of the city wall (2:9), which could well be the wall that Nehemiah built in 445 BC. Finally, the apocalyptic message of Joel 2:28–32 also favors a late date.[2] Our position in the commentary follows the postexilic dating.

---

1. Richard D. Patterson, "Joel," in EBC, Revised, Vol. 8 (Grand Rapids: Zondervan, 2008), 312.
2. David A. Hubbard, *Joel and Amos: An Introduction and Commentary*, TOTC (Downers Grove, IL: InterVarsity Press, 1989), 24.

HISTORICAL CONTEXT

The book of Joel is written in postexilic times when elders and priests, rather than kings and princes, are the leaders of the community (1:2, 13; 2:16–17).[3] Assyria and Babylonia are long gone. The book does not even mention the Northern Kingdom. The focus is on Judah and Jerusalem (3:1).

Jerusalem, where the temple is built, has become the center of worship since Josiah's reformation had destroyed all the local worship shrines at the high places (2 Kgs 23:1–15) and reinstated the celebration of the Passover (2 Kgs 23:23). After the siege of Jerusalem and the destruction of the temple in 586 BC, the people of God in exile fasted and recollected all the blessings they had enjoyed as free people. The liturgies of fasting, weeping, and mourning were ways for them to express their sorrow and grief before God. Following the assassination of Gedaliah, people come to the house of the Lord with offerings of grain and incense (Jer 41:4–5). This implies that worship services are being held. Just as Jeremiah had prophesied (Jer 31:6), Zion has become the center of worship (2:1, 15); worshipers are called the "people of Zion" (2:23) and it is "on Mount Zion and in Jerusalem" that the Lord will deliver his people (2:32).

Identifying Zion with Jerusalem follows a preexilic tradition dating back to David's victory over the Jebusites (2 Sam 5:7). Since the ark of the covenant was transferred from the city of Jerusalem to the temple, Zion is holy because the Lord dwells there (Ps 76:2; Isa 8:18). Joel also identifies Zion as the "holy hill" (2:1). The Lord will reign in Zion and Jerusalem (Isa 24:23). Following the postexilic prophet Zechariah on the theme of the Lord's defending Jerusalem (Zech 14:3), Joel also affirms God's protection over Zion and Jerusalem (3:16–17).

It is possible that the locust invasion takes place when the Judeans return to Jerusalem after 538 BC and that this fulfills the warning of Amos that locusts would devour their fig and olive trees (Amos 4:9). While Haggai's reference to a poor harvest and drought (Hag 1:6, 10–11) may describe the hardship of the Judeans as they return to Jerusalem, this could also be the result of the locust invasion (Joel 1:2–4; 2:25). The prophets Haggai and Zechariah exhort the Judean community to care for God's house (Hag 1:9, 14; Zech 1:16); the rebuilding of "the house of the LORD" (1:9, 14; 3:18) is finished in 515 BC.

---

3. Though for its placement between two preexilic prophets Hosea and Amos in the Hebrew canon may place the dating earlier, the scholarly consensus now shifted to the postexilic era. For a summary of discussion on the dating of Joel, see Raymond B. Dillard and Tremper Longman III, *An Introduction to the Old Testament* (Grand Rapids: Zondervan, 1994), 305–307.

Joel, like the postexilic prophets Haggai and Zechariah, directs the priests to call a sacred assembly in Zion (1:14; 2:15). Fasting was a common gesture of humility during the exilic and postexilic periods. God commanded them to fast (Zech 7:5; 8:19) as an expression of their humility, pain, and sorrow before the Lord. The priests play an important role in the restoration of the community (Zech 7:1–7; Neh 8:1–8). After the return from exile and the rebuilding of the temple, worship at the temple in Zion and Jerusalem became a reality.

AN ASIAN THEOLOGICAL READING OF JOEL

Elders as Leaders

Asian societies practice the Confucian virtue of filial piety. Elders are respected and old age is celebrated and honored. Elders preserve and pass on the family heritage by sharing their knowledge, experience, and insights with their children. The children, in turn, pass on this legacy to the next generation. In Asian cultures, it is natural for the younger generation to respect and defer to older people and authority figures. In the book of Joel, the elders are not only esteemed heads of families but also respected leaders in the community.

A Chinese saying goes, "A family with an old person has a living treasure of gold living with them" (*Jia you yi lao ru you yi bao*). To mark special occasions, Chinese families encourage intergenerational celebrations. Even married children are expected to return to their family of origin for these reunions, which are presided over by a patriarch or matriarch who holds the extended family together, strengthening family bonds and making families more cohesive. In Joel, the message of the locust plague is given first to the elders, and they are expected to pass on this message to as many as four generations (1:2–4).

Having instructed the priests to mourn and declare a holy fast, Joel tells them to summon the elders to the house of the Lord (1:13–14). The elders in the community were responsible for policy-making and for the welfare of the people. Their ideas shaped the plans and goals of the community. As respected figures in the community, elders were able to pass on important information to members of the community. When Joel wants to convene the entire community for a "sacred assembly," he first mentions the elders (2:16). The words of the elders carry weight among their families and clans. When a community respects its elders, these elders can have a greater influence and impact.

In Asian societies, elders exercise considerable authority and enjoy the respect of their families. This gives them many opportunities to lead family members to a saving relationship with our Lord Jesus, as well as to model and encourage faithfulness to Christ. By the example of their own walk with God, elders can both teach their family and their community about faith and model holy living.

Shame and Fear

The Asian culture is an honor and shame culture, and it is also a power and fear culture. The honor and shame worldview seeks to emphasize honor and eliminate shame. The power and fear worldview looks for ways to eradicate any perceived fear in the community. When there is fear, a society needs power to overcome various kinds of fear.

It is sometimes assumed that the Eastern concept of shame is an alternative to the Western idea of guilt. But for the Chinese community – and other societies that are influenced by Confucian values – shame is not an alternative to guilt. Shame helps to maintain social harmony in a culture.[4] The motivation for harmonious relationships in a group-oriented culture promotes the proper behavior of individuals.[5]

In the postexilic period in which Joel prophesies, shame has a positive value for the returnees.[6] The locust plague and drought prevent the people of God from enjoying a good harvest, and so they have no offerings to bring to God's house of worship (1:6–9). The farmers "despair" – and would experience shame – because the wine and the vine have "dried up" (1:10–12).[7] For the priests, the privilege and joy of serving God has turned to shame because they can no longer render service at the temple (1:13). The people also experience shame because they are unable to offer sacrifices at the temple (1:16).[8] To restore honor for the farmers, the vine growers, the priests, and the people, the community must acknowledge their shameful situation and change their wrongful behavior. Their shame draws them closer to the Lord (1:19–20).

Joel also uses the concept of honor and shame when appealing to the Lord to intervene on behalf of his people. When the enemies of God's people

---

4. Jin Li, Lianqin Wang, and Kurt W. Fisher, "The Organization of Chinese Shame Concepts," *Cognition and Emotion* 18 (2004): 767–797.
5. Patrick Chan Yi-Sang, "Romans 8 and the Chinese Concept of Shame and Guilt," *MissioDei: A Journal of Missional Theology and Praxis* 11(2020). See http://missiodeijournal.com/issues/md-11/authors/md-11-chan, accessed October 5, 2020.
6. Bin Kang, "The Positive Value of Shame for Post-exilic Returnees in Ezra/Nehemiah," OTE 33 (2020): 250–265.
7. Hubbard, *Joel and Amos*, 50.
8. Ronald A. Simkins, "'Return to Yahweh': Honor and Shame in Joel," *Semeia* 68 (1994): 47–48.

mock their situation (2:17), this is tantamount to disparaging God – for it is an attack against God's honor. The priests are God's ministers and the people are his inheritance. So their shame is tantamount to *his* shame because the nations will perceive his inaction in not defending his people as weakness. But Joel affirms that God will surely intervene and not allow his people to remain an object of scorn (2:19). God's promise of restoration is also an assurance that his people will receive honor and not shame (2:26–27). The invasion of his land and the scattering of his people among the nations is a disgrace to the Lord (3:1–8). God will execute justice against the nations and, thereby, both his people's honor and his own honor will be restored (3:12–17).

The locust plague and drought instill fear in the community (1:2–12). The people must cry to the Lord their God (1:19–20). As the fearful day of the Lord is announced, they must repent and humbly return to the Lord (2:12–13), who commands a powerful army (2:11). Crying out to the Lord is not merely an emotional release in the face of fear but a way to commit all fears to him. The Lord responds with words of comfort and assurance (2:20–25). He will fight for his people, defeat and judge their enemies, and be a refuge for his people (3:9–13, 16).

Creator and Sustainer

In Asia, there is seldom a need to prove the existence of God. Asian society is pluralistic, believing in multiple spirits and gods, and having many forms of worship and various houses of worship. Many people worship, in fear, a deity whom they view as an angry, unreasonable, or difficult to please. In contrast, Joel portrays the God of Israel as both Creator and Sustainer of his people.

The book of Joel describes a great and mighty God who uses the locust invasion to present his message of salvation to his people (1:2–4). The locust plague not only brings discomfort to the people but disrupts their lives. They can no longer enjoy the produce of the land (1:12). It also disrupts their ability to worship the Lord through their grain offerings and drink offerings (1:9). God is not unmindful of his people's suffering. He is even aware that the cattle and sheep are suffering (1:18). It is time for the people to call on the Creator who cares for his creation. If even the wild animals pant for God, how much more should the people of God pray to him (1:19–20)?

The Creator God not only oversees what is happening in his world, he sustains his creatures – both human beings and animals – by the provision of food. He not only creates but owns his creation and creatures. So the locusts are his army (2:25); they attack his land (1:6), his vines and fig trees (1:7). The people who suffer are his people and his inheritance (2:17; 3:2–3). As they repent, he will bless them so that they will know that he is their God (2:21). He will deliver them as they call on him (2:32). Although he roars from Zion, he will be a refuge for his own people (3:16–17). Even with so many agricultural disasters in Asia – brought about by natural calamities such as earthquakes, volcano eruptions, tsunami and flooding – the people of God can continue to trust in God, who controls the natural forces. He is their everlasting refuge and shield, proving to the unbelieving world that those who call upon his name can bounce back to life and health after each calamity.

THEOLOGICAL THEMES

Faithful God

God is sovereign over his people and there are no other gods before him (2:27; 3:17). He cares about the devastation that has befallen his people. In addition, God is jealous for his land and has mercy on his people (2:18). As the nations mock his people, his loving inheritance, God promises to intervene on their behalf. He will provide "grain, new wine and olive oil" for them and deliver them from their enemies (2:19–20). God will vindicate his name by judging the nations that have scattered his people and divided his land (3:2). The eschatological (future) judgment day concerns God's inheritance – "my people Israel" (3:2) – and is a decisive judgment rendered at the valley of Jehoshaphat (which means "the Lord judges"). The roaring of the Lord from Zion announces judgment for the nations but deliverance for his people (3:16).

Forgiving God

God is the sovereign Lord, yet he has compassion on his people. Through Joel, he invites the people to mourn, wail, fast, and appeal to him as their Lord (1:13; 2:12, 15–16). He is a forgiving God, who listens to their prayers of lament (1:19–20; 2:17) and responds with grace and compassion. When the people return to him and trust him with all their hearts, he reveals his steadfast love by relenting from his wrath, taking pity on his people, and blessing them (2:13, 18–19). God promises his Spirit and his presence to his people, enabling them to call on his name and enjoy the blessings of salvation (2:28–32; 3:17–18).

UNITY

The eschatological passages of the book are integral to its message. The book as a whole is symmetrical, with two parallel climaxes: "Then you will know that I am in Israel, that I am the LORD your God" (2:27) and "then you will know that I, the LORD your God, dwell in Zion, my holy hill" (3:17). The problem of devastation (1:4–20) is resolved by promised restoration (2:21–27). Repentance (2:12–17) results in blessing (2:28–32). And the judgment theme (2:1–11) finds a parallel in the final chapter (3:1–17).

The language of Joel presents a unified message. Two distinct units form a coherent whole: The first section (1:1–2:27) describes the theme of destruction, while the second (2:28–3:21) presents the theme of restoration. As the locusts that invaded Judah will be judged and extinguished, so the armies of nations that brought devastation will be defeated and judged.

USE OF TORAH AND PROPHETIC TRADITION

Joel follows the form of address used in Deuteronomy, where Moses commands the people of God to listen carefully. Moses wanted the people to pay careful attention and respond in obedient faith (Deut 5:1; 6:4; 9:1; 20:3). In chapter 1, Joel calls attention to the devastating effects – famine and drought – of the locust invasion. The portrayal of the awful day of the Lord in Joel would produce terrifying plagues. Both past events and upcoming plagues of locusts and drought are signs from the Lord for them to return to him.

Joel follows the prophetic tradition in several ways. First, in Joel 2:27 and 3:17, he uses Ezekiel's recognition formula, "Then you will know that I am the Sovereign LORD" (Ezek 13:23), combining this with Isaiah's explicit monotheism: "I am the LORD, and there is no other" (Isa 45:5).

Second, Joel follows the prophetic tradition concerning the day of the Lord as judgment, as first set forth in Amos, the first of the preexilic prophets.[9] Originally, Israel had viewed this as a day when the Lord came out to battle against Israel's foes, an understanding that arose out of their experience of God as the divine warrior in Exodus, leading his people out of Egypt (15:3–18).[10] But Amos reverses this meaning – seeing it as the day the Lord has come out against his people (5:18–20). For Zephaniah, the day is a day of distress and

---

9. See J. S. Wright, "Day of the Lord," in NBD, 3rd edition, ed. D. R. W. Wood (Leicester, UK: Inter-Varsity Press, 1996), 261.
10. For other possible theories on the origin of "the day," see James L. Crenshaw, *Joel: A New Translation with Introduction and Commentary*, AYBC (New Haven: Yale University Press, 1995), 47 fn 86.

anguish (1:14–18). Since God's judgment has a divine purpose, Joel refers to this day as a time of decision for God's people (3:14). Amid trouble for the nations, this would be a time of deliverance for those who revered God (Mal 4:1–2).

Third, in the face of enormous devastation, Joel preaches a message of repentance. The "return to the Lord" theme of Joel resembles the prophetic message of the eighth-century prophets (2:12–14; Hos 14:2; Amos 4:6–11). The command to "rend your heart" alludes to Hosea's image of a bear robbed of her cubs tearing open the body of her enemy (2:13; Hos 13:8; compare Hos 7:14).[11]

Finally, on a smaller scale, Joel 3 follows the prophetic tradition in prophesying judgment against the nations (Jer 46–51; Ezek 25–32). God will surely judge the nations for their evil deeds against his people.

NEW TESTAMENT CONNECTIONS

The NT appeals or alludes to Joel on several occasions. Most notably, on the day of Pentecost, Peter cites Joel's prophesy about the outpouring of the Holy Spirit in the last days (2:28–32; Acts 2:17–21).

Joel's call to humble repentance, to return to the Lord (1:13; 2:12–13), is a repeated theme in the NT, beginning with the preaching of John the Baptist (Matt 1:1–3). The call to "rend your heart and not your garments" (2:13) is similar to Paul's emphasis on circumcision of the heart (Rom 2:29).

The declaration that "everyone who calls on the name of the LORD will be saved" (2:32) is an important verse. It sheds light on the NT understanding of calling on the name of the Lord (Acts 4:9–12; 22:16; 1 Cor 1:2) and is directly quoted in Acts 2:21 and Romans 10:13. For the apostles, the only name by which a person may be saved is the name of Jesus Christ our Lord.

The "day of the LORD" (1:15; 2:1, 11, 31; 3:14) anticipates the future eschatological judgment, and Jesus and the NT writers frequently refer to this day. Jesus describes it as being the day of the Lord's judgment and emphasizes the uncertainty of its timing as well as the necessity to be in a constant state of preparedness (Matt 24:1–51; 25:31–46; Mark 13:1–37). Paul refers to this day in terms of "God's wrath" (Rom 2:5), "the Day" on which all deeds will be judged (1 Cor 3:13), and stresses the importance of being "pure and blameless"

---

11. There is a scholarly consensus that Joel should be studied within the context of the Twelve Minor Prophets, see Aaron Schart, "The First Section of the Book of the Twelve Prophets: Hosea-Joel-Amos," *Int* 61 (2007): 138–152.

(Phil 1:10). This day of the Lord will come unexpectedly, "like a thief in the night" (1 Thess 5:2), and will be accompanied by cosmic signs (2 Pet 3:10).

The book of Revelation also contains allusions to Joel in its use of imagery connected with the day of the Lord: the destroying army of locusts (1:6; 2:2–5; Rev 9:7–11); cosmic signs of the last days (2:10, 31; 3:15; Rev 6:12–14; 8:12); and the trumpet and sickle, which are symbols of judgment associated with the end times (2:1; 3:13; Rev 8:6; 14:15).

OUTLINE

1:1–2:17   **The Lord's Invitation to the People of God**

    1:1–20   First Lament: Impact of the Locust Plague

        1:1–12   Crisis: A Call for Preparation

        1:13–20   Response: A Call for Penitence and Prayer

    2:1–17   Second Lament: Impact of the Invading Army

        2:1–11   Crisis: A Call for Preparation

        2:12–17   Response: A Call for Penitence and Prayer

2:18–3:21   **The Lord's Blessings on the People of God**

    2:18–27   The Response of God

    2:28–32   The Renewal of God's People

    3:1–21   The Restoration of God's People

        3:1–8   God's Judgment

        3:9–17   God's Victory

        3:18–21   God's Blessing

JOEL 1:1–2:17

THE LORD'S INVITATION TO THE PEOPLE OF GOD

We must observe what is happening both in our region and in our world. In the year 2020, a strange and dangerous coronavirus named COVID-19 caught the global community off guard. It posed a serious threat to life and resulted in total lockdowns in many cities around the world. Coronaviruses are a family of viruses which cause not only the common cold but also more severe infections such as Severe Acute Respiratory Syndrome (SARS), Middle East Respiratory Syndrome (MERS), and, most recently, COVID-19 – which first appeared in late 2019 in Wuhan, China, and is transmitted through human-to-human contact. At the date of writing, there were more than 4.1 million cases of COVID-19 and at least 282,000 deaths.[1]

Around February 2020, swarms of desert locusts devastated crops and pasturelands in Somalia, Kenya, South Sudan, Uganda, and other parts of East Africa. The potential for famine and death is a frightening possibility for millions of people in that part of the world. Among migratory pests, desert locusts are the most dangerous. Experts say that multiple cyclones off Africa's east coast, producing heavy rains, helped the locusts to breed freely. The swarms of desert locusts may look like clouds on the horizon but, as they move closer and closer, instead of the hoped-for rain for their crops, farmers are left devastated by the destruction these locusts cause. One square kilometer swarm can contain about 40 million locusts; they can consume as much food a day as it takes to feed 35,000 people. According to experts, the worst is yet to come with the next rainy season – just as farmers get ready to plant – effectively enabling the breeding of a new generation of locusts. These locust swarms – aptly described as being "of biblical proportions" – recall not only the locust plague of Exodus (10:1–20) but also the message of Joel. The book of Joel has two main parts. In the first part, Joel uses the destruction caused by

---

1. Joshua Berlinger, Julia Hollingsworth, Zamira Rahim, and Adam Renton, "Coronavirus pandemic: Updates from around the world," see https://www.cnn.com/world/live-news/coronavirus-pandemic-05-11-20-intl/index.html, accessed May 11, 2020.

the locust plague to speak to the people (1:1–2:17). In the second, he speaks of God's promise of restoration (2:18–3:21). As a postexilic prophet, Joel uses the devastating effects of the locust plague to challenge the Judean community to fast and pray (1:1–20). This community of returnees is small in number. As Joel looks to the invading army that will herald the day of the Lord, he repeats the call to fast, pray, and return to the Lord (2:1–17).

1:1–20 FIRST LAMENT: IMPACT OF THE LOCUST PLAGUE

As a prophet, Joel is God's messenger. His message carries weight because it is God's word, backed by God's authority. Joel delivers a solemn message to Judah. The approaching "day of the LORD" (1:15; 2:1, 11, 31; 3:14) is no ordinary day but a catastrophic and dreadful day, and so the prophet encourages the people to pray (1:19; 2:17). While exhorting Judah to return to the Lord, the climax of Joel's message is an affirmation that the people will know that the Lord is indeed their God (2:27; 3:17).

The worldview of the OT is an integrated one. The Lord is viewed as being in charge of everything, including natural disasters. He is seen as being at work both in nature and in human history. The exilic prophets Jeremiah and Ezekiel proclaimed that the defeat by the Babylonians in 586 BC was no ordinary destruction but a chastisement from God. The eighth-century prophet Hosea proclaimed that catastrophe was directly connected with the sin of the people (Hos 4:1–3) and was a judgment from God upon his people (2:9, 12–13). In contrast to preexilic and exilic prophets who linked judgment with sin, Joel does not focus on the people's sin but uses the crisis of the locust plague as a basis for his message. He uses the extraordinary day of disaster (1:2) to add emphasis to his announcement of the day of the Lord (2:1–2) – a day that is not only near but even more dreadful, and which comes from the Lord (1:15).

The literary structure of Joel 1:1–20 is paralleled by that of Joel 2:1–17. First, there is the recurring motif of the day. It is a day of devastation. The crisis that comes through the locusts (1:2–12) is a harbinger of the dreadful day of invasion by an army headed by the Lord (2:1–11). Second, there is a repeated call to the people to humble themselves before God through weeping, mourning, and fasting (1:13–18; 2:12–17a), concluding with a prayer committing the matter to the Lord (1:19–20; 2:17b). Observe the resemblances between Joel 1:1–20 and Joel 2:1–17:

	Joel 1:1–20	Joel 2:1–17
Crisis: Call for Preparation	Day of disaster (1:1–12)	Day of disaster (2:1–11)
Response: Call for Penitence and Prayer	Need to weep, wail, and fast (1:13–18) A simple prayer (1:19–20)	Need to fast, weep, and mourn (2:12–17a) A simple prayer (2:17b)

God's judgment of his people reveals his sovereignty over the natural world, for it is his land, his vines, and his fig tree (1:6–7). He is the owner of the land and its crops (Lev 25:23). The prophet's message is addressed to the elders and to all who live in the land (1:2). Joel understands the heart of the Lord, and urges the people to lament before him. He uses the locust plague – an appalling natural disaster that devours every growing thing – to teach and instruct them.

1:1–12 Crisis: A Call for Preparation

Joel's oracle begins with the command to "hear" and to "listen" (1:2). The command to "hear" appears repeatedly in the book of Deuteronomy as Moses urges the people to pay careful attention (Deut 5:1; 6:4; 9:1; 20:3). Pairing the verbs "hear" and "listen" (literally, "give ear") emphasizes the importance of paying careful attention (Isa 28:23; Jer 13:15). Eighth-century prophets commonly prepared the people for their message by prefacing their utterances with the word "hear" (Isa 1:2; Hos 5:1; Amos 3:1; 4:1; 5:1; Mic 1:2; 3:9). Such similarities of language with these prophets might be one reason Joel is placed between Hosea and Amos.

The impact of the locust plague is widespread and a cause for grave concern. The natural catastrophe generates an ecological crisis. With crops destroyed, food is in short supply, affecting both animals and people. Joel first addresses the elders, the senior members of the community (1:2; compare 1:14; 2:16). This probably reflects the situation after the return from exile when there were no kings to provide leadership in the community: prophets share divine visions, priests provide teaching, and elders give counsel and shape policy (Jer 18:18; Ezek 7:26). The elders, as the community's well-respected guardians, would typically gather at the city gate to make decisions and resolve community disputes. As in many Asian societies, the elders function as community leaders; in the absence of a king, they also serve as spiritual leaders for God's people (1:14).

Joel stresses that everyone is affected by the locust invasion (1:2, 14). Just as with the locust plague in Egypt, the message must be passed on from one generation to the next (Exod 10:1–2); and everyone in the community has a duty to hand down truth by retelling this extraordinary event that has taken place in their midst. The message to trust God is relevant for all generations. Joel mentions four generations. The first generation, who experience this event, are commanded to tell it to their children, who, in turn, must convey it to the next generation and so on (1:3). As far back as patriarchal times, people passed on the faith of their fathers to the next generation by retelling their "stories" to their children and grandchildren. In the OT, the people of God are specifically commanded to do this. The story of God's saving acts is told and retold as good news in each generation, so that the people will remember and respond in worship (Exod 12:26–27; Deut 4:9–10). In Psalm 78, a generation that knows God and has experienced his love (78:1–3) determines to share their faith story with the next generation so that they, too, would know and obey God's word and faithfully pass on the faith to future generations (78:4–8).

Joel's prophecy is given in the context of God's covenant with Israel, a covenant that included both blessings and curses (Deut 28). The promise of covenantal blessings encouraged faithfulness to God. The threat of covenantal curses – which included warnings about plagues of locusts that would devour the crops, cutting off food supplies (Deut 28:38–42) – was intended to prompt people to return to God. Joel is urging the people to appreciate the gravity of God's actions and the urgency of turning back to him. The ecological crisis serves as a call to return to the Lord.

Locusts travel in swarms and cause terrible damage to crops. In an agricultural society, reliant on farming and herding, a locust attack would not simply disrupt but could completely destroy the life of the people; if locusts devoured all the crops and plants, both animals and people would starve. The 2020 locust swarms in East Africa bring to life the imagery Joel uses.

The use of four different Hebrew words for "locusts" (1:4) have been understood in two ways. The first is to see this as representing the four stages in the life cycle of the locust: pupa, adult, wingless larva, and winged larva. After the adult locusts lay their eggs, the eggs hatch to form a new generation that is 20 times larger than the previous one. Thus the population of desert locusts can increase exponentially. These dreaded pests can devour crops and pasturelands in a matter of hours. The locust outbreaks and upsurges in the Horn of Africa triggered widespread devastation of crops.[2]

The second way is to see the four different words for locusts as depicting the comprehensiveness of the destruction. The words "left" and "eaten" are repeated three times to show how widespread the devastation is. Like the plague of locusts associated with the exodus event (Exod 10:4–6, 12–15), this plague is also the work of God. In the OT worldview, natural disasters are considered acts of God, which represent an expression of his judgment. A natural disaster is believed to occur because of the sin of the people who willfully defy God (Hos 4:3). The OT views the world holistically. God is also the Creator, who is Lord over nature. When he judges his people, the natural environment is also affected (Hos 2:9, 12–13). Joel, however, does not explicitly connect the locust plague with sin but uses the crisis to grab their attention.

The postmodern world tends to scoff at any suggestion of a divine connection with natural disasters, preferring to pin the blame on the actions of superpowers. Christians, on the other hand, have sometimes been quick to conclude that natural disasters are "punishments" from God. Joel describes the locust plague as God's judgment. But unless God's word clearly says so, we dare not make such an assumption.

So exhaustive is the devastation that no one remains unaware of it and everyone in the land is impacted by it. Joel makes pronouncements about the devastation and also vividly portrays its impact. Both actions reveal Joel's urgency to deliver God's message. Joel calls the drunkards to wake up and recognize their plight (1:5–8); then he describes the predicament of the priests, unable to make their offerings at the temple (1:9–10); and finally, he calls the farmers to despair over the state of their fields and crops (1:11–12).

The drunkards are the first to be affected by the calamity. In the OT, wine was seen as a blessing from God, and wine came from the vines that the farmers harvested from the land. Joel calls the drunkards to "wake up" (perhaps from a drunken stupor) and recognize what was happening; they are to "weep" and "wail" because of the great calamity that deprive them of God's blessing of new wine (1:5). The numerical and physical strength of the locusts is brought out by comparing them to a "nation" and a "mighty army"; the ferocity of the attack is conveyed by the metaphors of a "lion" and "lioness" (1:6). Vines

---

2. Madeline Stone, "A Plague of Locust has descended on East Africa. Climate Change may be to blame." See https://www.nationalgeographic.com/science/2020/02/locust-plague-climate-science-east-africa/, accessed February 19, 2020.

and figs trees were common in Israel and were symbols of God's blessing and peace (1:7; Hos 2:12; Mic 4:4). Hence, the destruction of the vines and fig trees was a reversal of divine blessing.

In light of these disasters (1:5–7), the prophet invites the drunkards to mourn. Judah is personified as a virgin. Mourning in sackcloth was an outward sign of mourning when there was a death in the family (compare Gen 37:34). In Israelite society, a betrothed virgin was regarded as a wife even though the marriage was not yet consummated. Mourning like a virgin describes the terrible grief of a young woman whose betrothed husband died before the marriage took place (1:8).

Joel then moves on to the predicament of the priests (1:9–10). Grain offerings and drink offerings were connected with the daily burnt offerings in the house of the Lord (1:9, 13; Exod 29:38–42). The ingredients for grain and drink offerings come from the ground. With the harvest in jeopardy, the priests are unable to minister properly before the Lord. Nor will they have enough for their own consumption (Lev 6:14–18). Therefore, they are in mourning. Joel commands them to put on sackcloth and mourn (1:13) and to lead the people in fasting and praying to the Lord (1:14).

Finally, Joel addresses the farmers (1:11–12). God had promised that his people would enjoy the blessings of grain, new wine, and oil in the land (Deut 7:13; 11:14). These were basic commodities in Israelite society: grain for sustenance, new wine for enjoyment, and oil for personal and religious use (Ps 104:15). The harvest was a joyous occasion, when farmers and vine growers would rejoice in the fruit of their labor. Because of the drought, the fields have dried up, the crops have failed, and the vines and fig trees have withered, and so has their joy (1:12).

Joel, as God's spokesman, tries to awaken the community to the gravity of their situation. Without the vines and fig trees, the drunkards have no wine to drink (1:5–8). With drought and famine, the priests have nothing for the temple offerings (1:9–10). With ruined fields, the farmers have no food to eat and enjoy (1:11–12). Because of this catastrophe, there is no food for nourishment, no fruits and wine for celebration, and nothing to offer for their worship. It is a complete disaster for the community!

The message of Joel challenges us to be sensitive to how God is speaking to us through calamities. First, calamities may be a call to repentance, to confess and change our sinful ways. Second, it is an opportunity to reorder our priorities and focus on what is truly important. COVID-19 and the "new normal" has helped many to recognize that money is not everything and that relationships are precious. Third, a crisis is a call to generous, compassionate, and responsible stewardship of the resources God has entrusted to us. In the aftermath of calamities, churches have been quick to respond to calls for assistance. During the early months of the COVID-19 crisis, a graduate student in clinical Christian counseling began distributing free brochures on "Emotional First Aid" to police officers, doctors, teachers, and parents. God's people, even when they themselves are experiencing adversities, are called to extend the comfort and compassion of Christ to those who are impoverished, both materially and spiritually. In times of calamity, Christians should look for opportunities to reach out in compassion.

1:13–20 Response: A Call for Penitence and Prayer

Joel links the locust plague with the day of the Lord (1:15). The catastrophe anticipates an even bigger destruction that comes from the Almighty himself! This calls for spiritual action. Penitence and prayer are essential. The people must turn to God. In this section, the prophet urges the people to prepare (1:13), to plead (1:14–18), and to pray (1:19–20).

This call to prayer (1:13–20) corresponds to a similar call to prayer in chapter two (2:12–17).

	Joel 1:13–20	Joel 2:12–17
Prepare	Call to penitence (1:13)	Call to penitence (2:12–14)
Plead	Call to fast and a sacred assembly (1:14–18)	Call to fast and a sacred assembly (2:15–17a)
Pray	Call to pray (1:19–20)	Call to pray (2:17b)

Joel calls the priests to mourn and wail. When they minister before the altar, the priests are ministering before the Lord (1:9, 13; 2:17), serving as leaders who lead the community to turn to God. The lack of grain and drink offerings hinders them in this role of mediating communion with God.

Just as the drunkards were exhorted to weep and wail (1:5) and God's people were invited to grieve like a virgin girding herself in sackcloth (1:8), the priests are now instructed to mourn and wail and spend the night in sackcloth (1:13). This was a call to deep contrition. Sackcloth was an outward expression of penitence and grief (1 Kgs 21:27; Neh 9:1–2) and expressed both humility and helplessness.

Joel expects the priests to take the lead in communal acts of repentance. He directs them to gather the elders and all the inhabitants of the land and proclaim a "holy fast" and summon a "sacred assembly" (1:14). While fasting meant refraining from eating, a sacred assembly – a special gathering of all God's people – required stopping all work. As leaders of the community, the elders were responsible for gathering all the people together. In the OT, fasts were commanded during times of crisis to encourage God's people to come before him in humility to repent, to lament, or to plead for deliverance (Judg 20:26; Jonah 3:5; Neh 1:4). To cry out in lament is a way of expressing helplessness, the way a baby cries out to its mother. The fasts were opportunities for God's people to collectively reflect on God's actions and cry out for help. A solemn assembly, on the other hand, was a corporate gathering for a specific purpose. While this could be a festive celebration, here it is part of a penitential response to the Lord (Neh 9:1–3).

The prophet wants the people to look beyond the seriousness of their present situation (1:16–18) to the gravity of the day of the Lord – a day of judgment and destruction by the Almighty (1:15). The purpose of Joel's announcement is to stress the nearness of the day and the need to prepare for it without delay. It was Amos who first presented "the day" as a day of destruction for the people of God (Amos 5:16–20; 6:3; 8:9). Joel links the event of the locust plague with this great event that will transpire in the future (2:1–2). The invading army is not merely a disaster but the fulfillment of what earlier prophets had spoken about, pointing to the eschatological day of the Lord (3:14–15).

The locust plague serves as a warning that the day of the Lord is imminent. The prophet points his hearers to the evidence of devastation around them: first, with no rains, there is a scarcity of food, leading to a lack of offerings for worship (1:16); second, with no harvest, the storehouses lie abandoned (1:17); and third, with no pasturelands, even the sheep and cattle are in distress (1:18).

Joel offers a framework for prayer for the priests to use as they lead the congregation in prayer before the Lord (1:19–20).[3] This is not just any cry but

---

3. James Crenshaw, Douglas Stuart, and Joel Joseph point to the prophet Joel as the intercessor. James L. Crenshaw, *Joel*, 110; Douglas Stuart, *Hosea-Jonah*, WBC (Waco, TX: Word, 1987), 244; Joel Joseph, "Joel" in SABC (Carlisle: Langham, 2015), 1132. John Barton, however, argued that the lament speaker in the community utters the prayer. John Barton, *Joel and Obadiah*, OTL (Louisville: Westminster John Knox Press, 2001), 83.

a lament. Joel believes that a complaint made direct to God about the devastation in God's land will result in God's action. The drought and the intense heat have ravaged the pasturelands and fields, probably compounding the risk of fire. The streams have dried up and even the wild animals have no water to drink. Joel emphasizes all these calamities to motivate the priests and elders to take urgent action by gathering the people to collectively call on the Lord in prayer. Calamity is reversible when God's people humble themselves and pray.

In Asian societies which are guided by Confucianism elders tend to focus on self-preservation and saving face. The stress on harmonious relationships and the desire to avoid unpleasantness may lead to covering up rather than dealing with issues. Joel is countercultural in his approach. Although the locust plague brings destruction and shame, the incident is not something to be forgotten and buried. He exhorts the elders to retell the story to their children and to their children's children (1:2–4). Future generations not only need to remember the calamities that have befallen the community but pass on to the next generation the spiritual lessons learned through these difficult times. And the elders, along with the people, must cry out to the Lord in humble repentance (1:13–14). Joel models how leaders with a spiritual thirst for God can motivate the community, including future generations, to return to the Lord and to call upon him in prayer. The prophet even provides them with a framework for prayer (1:19–20).

2:1–17 SECOND LAMENT: IMPACT OF THE INVADING ARMY

2020 was a year of extraordinary disasters around the globe. The year began with bushfires in Australia, followed by floods in Indonesia and Korea. With the US-Iran conflict, a Ukrainian passenger plane was blown to pieces. Philippines was shaken by numerous earthquakes. Locust swarms invaded Yunan in China, as well as many parts of Africa, the Arabian Peninsula, and the Middle East.

At the time of writing (March 2020), farmers in East Africa are planting their crops amid threats of a second wave of locusts. Unusual climatic conditions have enabled the desert locust to multiply rapidly. The rainy season will likely aggravate the situation. Desert locusts are active and voracious, and farmers are hoping desperately that the helicopters spraying pesticides are as mobile as the locusts. The supply of pesticides is hindered by the closing of national borders due to the COVID-19 outbreak. Famines are expected. Both the locust plagues and the COVID-19 pandemic remind us of the day of the Lord. As in Joel's time, pestilence and disease can serve as a call to come humbly before our Lord and listen to his message. The prophecies of Joel continue to be relevant today.

Is the locust destruction in Joel a past event or a present one? Is it a real event or just a metaphor? Traditionally, there have been three schools of thought about how the mention of locusts in chapters 1 and 2 (1:4; 2:25) should be interpreted.

In the first interpretation, the locust plague (1:4) and invasion (2:25) are interpreted metaphorically, as attacks by human enemies. These attacks are God's judgment against disobedient Israel.[4]

A second interpretation sees the first as an actual locust plague (1:4) and the second as a military attack. Both are results of God's judgment against the nation.

A third interpretation sees the first locust plague (1:4) as an actual event, a judgment that has already taken place, which is then used as a metaphor to depict the havoc that will take place in the future on the day of the Lord.[5]

This commentary follows the third interpretation. Joel 1 describes a local catastrophe with real locusts (1:4) that has already taken place, while Joel 2:1–17 describes an impending disaster on a universal scale. The prophet Joel uses the past event of the devastation of the locust plague to call attention to a forthcoming event of even greater magnitude. The day of the Lord is imminent. The people must prepare. As the people humbly lament, the Lord promises restoration and blessing (2:27).

2:1–11 Crisis: A Call for Preparation

The call for preparation is directly linked to the day of the Lord. The twin motifs of the day of the Lord (2:1, 11) and darkness (2:2, 10) bracket the description of the devastation that will take place on this day. The prophet uses highly figurative language to convey the terror of the widespread destruction. This is intended to move the people to take corrective action before it is too late. Joel develops the theme of God's impending judgment as he moves from the historical locust plague to the coming devastation by the invading army.

Zion, God's holy hill, is a dominant theological theme in Joel. It was once the Jebusites' fortress. After conquering the Jebusites, David renamed Zion the "city of David" (2 Sam 5:6–9). Since the temple was located on this holy

---

4. Stuart, *Hosea-Jonah*, 233–234.
5. Barton, *Joel and Obadiah*, 44–47, 67–68; David Baker, *Joel, Obadiah, Malachi*, NIVAC Old Testament (Grand Rapids: Zondervan, 2006), 55.

hill, reference to Zion points to God's dwelling and activity (Pss 3:4; 48:1–3). Because of its elevation, Zion was ideally suited to sound a warning (2:1) or to summon God's people to worship (2:15). Zion was the place of God's deliverance (2:32) as well as his judgment (3:16), and it will be his eternal dwelling place with his people (3:17, 21).

Joel uses two imperatives – "blow the trumpet" and "sound the alarm" – that warn about the approaching day of the Lord (2:1). A trumpet referred to a ram's horn or *shofar*, sometimes used to summon the people to worship but also used as a battle cry (Judg 3:27; 6:34) or as a warning of imminent danger (Hos 8:1; Amos 3:6). Watchmen on the walls of Jerusalem would sound the alarm by blowing a trumpet to warn the people of the approach of the enemy. As a prophet, Joel serves as God's watchman, sounding a warning about the upcoming disaster and warning God's people to prepare for God's judgment. The prophet's message is theocentric, linking the day of the Lord with the Lord as the head of his mighty army (2:1, 11; compare 1:15).

Joel introduced the theme of the day of the Lord in 1:15. He returns to it and elaborates on it in 2:1–11. He begins by warning that the day is "close at hand" (2:1) and concludes with a sobering description of this "dreadful" day (2:10–11). In Hebrew, the "day" is not always a literal twenty-four-hour time period but a way to express temporal rhythms that are packed with meaningful content. The day of the Lord is an interruption, an unexpected intervention of God when his enemies were sure they were winning. When it arrives, it will alter the present course of history.

As God pours out his wrath on his enemies on the day of the Lord (2:1–2; Amos 5:18–20; Zech 1:14–15), this day becomes a day of blessing for his people (3:9–21; Hos 2:18–23; Amos 9:11–15). For God's enemies, then, it is a "day of darkness and gloom" (2:2), a day of distress, anguish, trouble, and ruin (Zeph 1:15). But now the tables have been turned: it is Judah and Jerusalem who face darkness and destruction. God has come against them as if they were his enemies (2:2–11).

The day of the Lord comes like an invading army that leaves a trail of destruction in its wake (2:2b–9). There is great darkness and gloom, as when dark clouds cover the earth before a thunderstorm (2:2a). The Lord's large and mighty army advances like a forest fire that devours everything in sight. The land that had once flourished like the garden of Eden is now laid bare, a desert waste (2:2b–3). What a terrifying contrast! Compared to the devastation caused by the locust army (1:2–4, 16–19), this destruction is greater in both intensity and scope.

Joel uses several metaphors to describe the appearance and actions of this army. They are swift, like soldiers galloping on horseback, leaping over obstacles with terrifying noises as they charge to do battle (2:4–5; Judg 5:22; Nah 3:2). The sight of this invading army terrifies the nations – "every face turns pale" (2:6). The warriors are swift, strong, skilled, disciplined, and relentless in their attack (2:7–9). The cosmic disturbances described are evidence that the Lord himself is coming, leading this mighty army (2:10–11a). "The day of the LORD is great; it is dreadful. Who can endure it?" (2:11b). The answer is, no one! The only way to avert this disaster is to repent and return to the Lord (2:12–17).

2:12–17 Response: A Call for Penitence and Prayer

Just as in chapter 1, the call to prepare is followed by a call for penitence and prayer. The prophet's call to put on sackcloth and mourn is mirrored by the call to return to the Lord (1:13; 2:12–14), while the command to declare a fast and summon a sacred assembly to lament before the Lord is also repeated (1:14; 2:15–17). In both instances, the priests are to lead the people in prayer (1:13; 2:17). Return to the Lord is possible because of his invitation (2:12), his compassionate nature (2:13), his desire to bless (2:14), and his readiness to listen and answer his people's prayers (2:15–17).

How should we interpret the call to return to the Lord? Is this a call to ask for forgiveness, a call to turn to God in times of trouble, or is there some other reason? One view assumes that since the sins of the people are not elaborated and Joel does not rebuke sin, this is simply a call to turn to God for help in a crisis.

A second view argues that the people have sinned and are under punishment. So they need to repent and return to God in order to receive his blessings. This is a call to a renewal. This is the covenantal model of sin-punishment-repentance-blessing.

A third view interprets the call to return from the perspective of the honor-shame model. Accordingly, it is not that the sins of the people caused the judgment but that the disaster and the derision against the Lord brought shame to the Lord. Therefore, the call to return to the Lord summons people to grieve because the Lord has been dishonored. As they do this, God would act to reverse the situation by bringing calamity upon those who caused calamity to his people and thus restore his honor among both his people and his enemies.

The authors believe that the call to return to the Lord involves all these things and more. It is turning to God in a crisis and trusting in him, as well as turning to him with repentant hearts and changed behavior. The eighth-century prophet Hosea exposes the sins of the people (Hos 4:1–5; 5:4–7) before urging them to return to the Lord (6:1–3); Amos also brings indictments against the people (Amos 4:1–5) before expanding on the warning signs of famine, drought, hunger, plagues, and war which were intended to prompt the people to return to the Lord (4:6–11). Although Joel does not list their specific sins, the postexilic community, sensitive to the teaching of the Torah, would have interpreted plagues, famine, and drought as warnings to repent and return to the Lord (Deut 28:23–24, 38). God had already made provision for his people to seek forgiveness (1 Kgs 8:22, 35–39). Now he speaks in the first person, urging the community to return to him before it is too late to avert the final devastation (compare Deut 30:1–3).

The people are urged, "return to me with your whole heart" (2:12) – in other words, their return must be wholehearted, with conviction, and without delay. In the OT, the heart reflects a person's inner character (1 Sam 16:7) and is the seat of the emotions (Judg 18:20; 1 Sam 1:8; Ps 39:3), the will (Prov 4:23), and the intellect (Ps 90:12). In the Torah, the people are called to seek and love God with all their heart (Deut 4:29; 6:5), and a circumcised heart is one that returns to him (Deut 10:16; compare Jer 9:26).

In view of the impending disaster, the whole community is asked to fast, weep, and mourn. These are progressive signs of a solemn lament. Lament is a humble and sincere expression of their disappointment and frustration. It is a faith that acknowledges sadness and their deep longing for the Lord. A person would tear his garment as a sign of heartrending misfortune or mourning (Gen 37:29; Num 14:6; 2 Sam 3:31; Isa 36:22). Here, God's people are invited to "rend your heart and not your garments" (2:13). The Lord is seeking inward contrition and not just an external show of piety. To rend the heart implies responding to the Lord with a broken and contrite heart (Ps 51:17).

Returning to the Lord is possible because he is "gracious and compassionate, slow to anger and abounding in love" (2:13b). All these adjectives describe the gracious character of God, first revealed to Moses at Mount Sinai (Exod 34:6–7) and which had become a creedal statement about God's attributes (Num 14:18; Neh 9:17; Jonah 4:2). Nevertheless, God's compassion and mercy do not negate his commitment to bring about justice. His righteousness demands that iniquity be punished.

Relenting is an interesting facet of God's character. When people come to him with truly penitent hearts, God "relents from sending calamity" (2:13c; Exod 32:14; Jonah 3:9–10). The converse, however, is also true – those who reject God's mercy will experience his wrath (Jer 15:6). Joel, like Jonah, stresses God's compassionate love, which warns and punishes because he wants sinners to return to him. As the people return to God, he will "turn and relent" and bless them so that, in a reversal of their earlier situation (1:9, 13), they will be able to present grain and drink offerings to him (2:14).

The people must come before the Lord with prepared hearts. Seven imperative verbs direct how they are to prepare to receive grace and forgiveness from the Lord (2:15–16):

(1) *Blow* the trumpet
(2) *Declare* a holy fast
(3) *Call* a sacred assembly
(4) *Gather* the people
(5) *Consecrate* the assembly
(6) *Bring together* the elders
(7) *Gather* the children

Unlike the earlier call to blow the trumpet – as a warning of imminent disaster (2:1) – these commands call the people to humble themselves as they plead for deliverance. The people must not only gather together but purify themselves as they prepare to meet their God (compare Exod 19:10, 22). Their outward religiosity should reflect an inner transformation. The whole community is to gather, from elders to nursing babies. Even the bridegrooms – who were exempted from military duty (Deut 20:7; 24:5) – and brides were expected to join the assembly. The entire community must join in turning to the Lord, seeking his intervention and salvation.

The priests, the people's representatives before God, are commanded to weep. As leaders in the community, their ministry is not just to serve at the altar but also to lead the people in prayer before the Lord (2:17; compare 1:13). The place where they are to offer the prayer is between the temple porch and the altar of burnt offering. This means that the priests stand at the entrance to the temple building and then lead the people in a prayer of lament.

As in chapter 1, the prophet gives a simple framework for their prayer (2:17; compare 1:19–20). This brief prayer is one of genuine grief, heartfelt groaning, and a desperate cry for help. It consists of two petitions. The first – "Spare your people, LORD" – is a plea for mercy based on God's gracious character. In the second petition, the prophet says that God's absence causes his people to become "an object of scorn" in the sight of the nations and urges

God to act to defend his own honor. Following the OT lament tradition and postexilic penitential prayers, this prayer links the people's shame with God's honor.[6] The focus is not on the people's predicament but on God's ownership – "your people" and "your inheritance" are terms of endearment referring to those who belong to the Lord.

The word "inheritance" can mean the land allotted to God's people (Num 34:2; Deut 4:21). God owns the land (Lev 25:23), and so he must defend his inheritance. Here in Joel, however, the *people* are God's inheritance. They are the Lord's chosen possession and valuable heritage (2:17; Deut 9:26; Ps 28:9). The word "inheritance" emphasizes the certainty of ownership. His chosen people are his property and heritage. Their position as his chosen possession is secure. This prayer pleads with God to spare his own people lest they become a laughingstock before the neighboring nations.

"Where is their God?" occurs frequently in laments (Pss 42:10; 79:10). Joel cites a common argument: God's apparent absence would cause the surrounding nations to taunt God's people with the accusation that God had abandoned them. So the scorn poured out on his people is also a shame and disgrace to the Lord. The prayer appeals to God to intervene to defend his honor.

This section (2:12–17) parallels Joel 1:13–20. The people are to appeal directly to the Lord, who calls them to return to him. The priests who minister before the Lord are to lead the people with a prayer of lament. The pivotal message of Joel, which is found at the midpoint of the entire book, is that God's people should seek his intervention. God hears and responds to his people's prayers for restoration (Ps 80:3, 7, 19).

---

6. Jerry Hwang, "How Long will my Glory be Reproach?: Honour and Shame in Old Testament Lament Traditions," OTE 30 (2017): 684–706.

JOEL 2:18–3:21

THE LORD'S BLESSINGS ON
THE PEOPLE OF GOD

The Lord responds to his people's prayer of lament. Whereas the first part of the book uses the calamities of the locust plague and drought to invite the people to return to the Lord (1:1–2:17), the second part of the book contains messages of comfort, affirming the Lord's compassion and blessing on his people (2:18–3:21). When the people return to the Lord, he responds graciously, promising both material and spiritual blessings. His material blessings extend to the land, the animals, and the people (2:18–27). Spiritual blessings come in the form of the Spirit who will be poured out on all people (2:28–32) and in the restoration of the fortunes of Judah and Jerusalem (3:1–21). The restoration of God's people begins with the promise of God's judgment on Judah's enemies (3:1–8); with this victory, the people can live securely in the land as God dwells in their midst (3:9–21). There is a shift from gloom to hope. Both types of blessings result in God's dwelling among his people and their recognition that he is their God (2:27; 3:17). This second part of Joel has three main sections: (a) the response of God (2:18–27), (b) the renewal of God's people (2:28–32), and (c) the restoration of God's people (3:1–21).

There are close parallels between Joel 2:18–27 and Joel 3:1–12: the Lord's response is to act on behalf of his people (2:18–20; 3:1–3); the renewal God brings should prompt his people to celebrate (2:21–23; 3:4–8); and God's actions prompt recognition of who he is (2:24–27; 3:9–12). The table below shows these parallels:

	Joel 2:18–27	Joel 3:1–12
God's Response	Act on behalf of his people (2:18–20)	Act on behalf of his people (3:1–3)
People's Response	Celebrate (2:21–23)	Celebrate (3:4–8)
People's Recognition of God	He is the Lord (2:24–27)	He is the Warrior (3:9–12)

2:18–27 THE RESPONSE OF GOD

At the dedication of the first temple, God had spoken to Solomon about situations where God's people would face judgment in the form of drought, locust attacks, or plagues (2 Chr 7:13). If they humbly repented, God had promised to forgive their sins and heal their land (2 Chr 7:14). Joel 2:18–27 shows how God responds to his people's repentance by reversing judgment and bringing blessings. As they return to him, God reaffirms his commitment to his people and to his land (2:18). There will be rain; the land will be fruitful once more; the locusts will be driven away and the people's shame will be removed; and there will be rejoicing (2:19–26). There are two promises by God (2:18–20, 25–27) and a call to rejoice in his blessings (2:21–24). In response to the earlier taunt (2:17), the people will experience the presence of their God, the only true God, in Israel (2:27).

God is blessing his people and will restore what he has taken away. The restoration (2:18–27) includes all the elements devastated by the locust plague and drought (1:1–20).

	Restoration Joel 2:18–27	Devastation Joel 1:1–20
Grain	Grain restored (2:19, 24a)	Grain withheld (1:10–11, 17)
Animals	Food available (2:22a)	Food unavailable (1:18–20)
Fig and vine	Fruitful (2:22b)	Fruitless (1:7, 12)
Rain	Abundance (2:23)	Scarcity (1:12, 17)
New wine and oil	Overflow (2:24b)	Withheld (1:5, 10)
Locust	God will restore what the locusts have devoured (2:25)	Devoured (1:4)
People	Honor restored (2:26–27)	Shame (1:5, 9)

Both jealousy and pity will prompt the Lord to act to reverse the drought and famine (2:18). The Lord's jealousy is a divine attribute, enshrined in the covenant with his people. On the one hand, the Lord wants the people of God to serve only him (Exod 20:5; 34:14; Deut 5:9). He is a faithful God, jealous for his land and his people. To be jealous is an action verb that expresses God's passionate care for them (Ezek 39:25; Zech 1:14). Pity expresses God's compassion on his people as they undergo hardships and suffering.

When God's people obey, the Lord sends rain in its season (Deut 11:13–15). He grants blessings of grain, new wine, and olive oil in abundance (2:19) – the same commodities that were earlier destroyed (1:10). The shame that came from being scorned will be removed and God's people will not be disgraced again.

The Lord is jealous for his people. He demonstrates his love for them by defeating and driving away their enemies so that they can enjoy peace in the land (Deut 28:7). The locust is used as a metaphor for the northern army (2:20). The northern army, threatening and fearsome, appears in prophetic literature as the Lord's agent of destruction. Now that enemy will be driven away to the Dead Sea and the Mediterranean, far away from Israel's boundaries. As the warriors die, the stench will rise up from the corpses.

This oracle of God's salvation and grace is followed by the prophet's joyous response (2:21–24). Indeed, the Lord has done magnificent deeds for his people! All the earlier calamities will be reversed. God will restore more than he has taken away. The OT depicts an integrated world in which God controls everything, including the land and wild animals. Joel addresses the land (2:21), the wild animals (2:22), and the people of Zion (2:23). The land and the wild animals need not fear, for open pastures are becoming green, the trees are bearing fruit, the fig tree and the vine are yielding their produce, and the animals will have food (2:21–22; compare 1:10, 12, 20). These are signs of abundance and fruitfulness. The drought is now a thing of the past as God blesses the land.

As for the people of Zion, they will enjoy abundant showers (2:23; compare 1:10, 12, 20). In an agricultural society, timely rains result in a plentiful harvest (Jer 5:24). The autumn rains, also known as early rains, prepare the ground for plowing and sowing at the end of the dry season. The spring rains, also known as latter rains, provide the water required for the grain to grow. While Egypt depended on the Nile for water to irrigate their fields, in Judah, a good harvest depended on the rains in season. So the giving of the early and latter rains was sometimes interpreted theologically as God's blessings for those who faithfully keep his covenant (Deut 11:10–15; 28:12). The promise of autumn and spring rains signifies the resumption of all rains. With this blessing of rain, the threshing floors will be filled with grain and the vats will overflow with new wine and oil (2:24; compare 1:5, 17). The people will not only have plenty to eat but be fully satisfied (2:26a). The restoration affirms God's faithfulness.[1] The people of Zion should celebrate and praise his name because of the wonders he has done for them!

Not just the harvest (2:23–26a) but hope is also restored. The people will know the satisfaction of being delivered from shame (2:26b) and enjoying an intimate covenant relationship with God (2:27; Exod 6:7; Lev 26:12). The theology of God's presence is an important concept in the OT. It is part of God's covenantal blessing. When there is hardship and suffering, outsiders may interpret this as pointing to God's absence and they may mock God's people. But the Lord remains faithful to his promise to dwell among his people (Exod 6:7; 25:8); and he will make it known among his people and among the nations that he alone is the Lord (Isa 45:5–6, 14, 21–22).

2:28–32 THE RENEWAL OF GOD'S PEOPLE

This section describes another way in which the Lord responds to his people's repentance. The vivid descriptions in this section start with the Lord's promise about things to come. This will be a radical break from the past. In this new era, God promises to dispense his Spirit (2:28–29), display his power (2:30–31), and deliver his people (2:32).

This promise of God pouring his Spirit on people (2:28–32) can be compared with the promise of prosperity for God's people on the day of the Lord (3:13–21). The Lord will demonstrate his lordship as he pours out his Spirit on his people (2:28–29) and also as he gathers the nations for judgment on behalf of his people (3:13–14). Both prophecies speak of his supernatural cosmic signs (2:30–31; 3:15–17) and conclude on a note of hope, with a message of deliverance for God's people (2:32; 3:18–21).

---

1. NIV 2011 is correct in interpreting the giving of rain as his faithfulness – that is, God's righteousness. RSV and ESV, however, interpret the rain as a vindication for the people. God vindicates the people with the giving of the rains.

	Joel 2:28–32	Joel 3:13–21
The day of the Lord	The Lord pouring out his Spirit (2:28–29)	The Lord sitting in judgment (3:13–14)
Cosmic signs	The Lord showing his wonders (2:30–31)	The Lord roaring in judgment from Zion (3:15–17)
Deliverance	Message of hope (2:32)	Message of hope (3:18–21)

In the OT, the Spirit empowers leaders to fulfill their duties in various roles – for instance, as judges or deliverers (Judg 3:10), as prophets (1 Sam 10:6), and as kings (1 Sam 16:13). The gift of the Spirit is given so that God's purposes may be fulfilled (Exod 31:2–5; Zech 4:6).

The oracle of blessings points to a new era. The outpouring of the Spirit will be available for all people, regardless of age, gender, ethnicity, economic class, or social status. This is a new and splendid outpouring of God's Spirit, which will fulfill a wish expressed by Moses many centuries before (Num 11:29). The Spirit of God transforms and gives life to human beings (Gen 2:7). With the Spirit in their hearts, people will have both the willingness and the ability to walk with God and obey him (Ezek 36:26–27). In contrast to the outpouring of devastation in Joel 1, the outpouring of the Spirit transforms people and guarantees the Lord's favor.

Prophecy, dreams, and visions are interrelated terms, directly associated with God's revelation and prophetic activities. These were typical ways by which God enabled people, from the greatest to the least, to know him (Num 12:6; Jer 31:31–34; Ezek 26:27–28). But this was only possible because of God's Spirit. The initiative comes from God. Prophecies are verbal, whereas visions and dreams are visual.

It is the Spirit who inspires prophets and empowers them to prophesy (1 Sam 10:6, 10; Ezek 11:5; Mic 3:8). These prophecies, God's revelation, must be faithfully conveyed as God's word to his people (Jer 23:25–28). In the case of the writing prophets, the revelations received by them have been recorded as God's word. The prophets are the Lord's spokespersons. The messenger formula in the prophetic books clearly affirms that the prophet's message comes from God and that the test of a prophet's authenticity is the fulfillment of God's word (Deut 18:14–22).

Dreams also come from God. Even in earlier days, God spoke in dreams to Abimelech (Gen 20:3–7), Jacob (Gen 28:10–17; 31:10–13), Laban (Gen 31:24), and Joseph (Gen 37:5–11). But dreams need interpretation (Gen 41:1–8) and the ability to interpret them comes from God's Spirit (Gen 41:15–16, 38). God uses dreams to guide (Gen 28:10–17) or protect (Gen 31:10–13) his people. In some cases, dreams come to rebuke people (Gen 20:3–7). Likewise, visions also come from God (Gen 46:2–4). Visions strengthen the commitment to serve God (Isa 6:1; Jer 1:11–14; Ezek 1:1).

In addition to prophecies, dreams, and visions, God can use wonders in heaven and on earth to demonstrate his power and convey his message. Such signs also accompany the outpouring of the Spirit (2:30–31). The purpose of these celestial phenomena is to show God's concern for and involvement with his people. Such signs are visible both to the people of God and to the watching world (Exod 7:3; Deut 4:34; Ps 78:43). The darkening of the sun and the moon turning to blood are supernatural signs of cosmic upheaval, related to the day of the Lord (Rev 6:12). This day of the Lord's coming is both a day of salvation and a day of judgment. Terrifying signs precede that terrible day.

The purpose of these signs is to prompt people to call on the name of the Lord. In the OT, to call on God's name could mean acknowledging him as God (Gen 4:26), enjoying an intimate relationship with him (Gen 12:8), or praying for his help (2 Kgs 5:11). Calling on the name of the Lord implies trusting him for salvation; and deliverance comes when his name is invoked in faith. The NT refers to calling on the name of the Lord Jesus Christ in order to be saved (Acts 2:21; 22:16; Rom 10:13).

Joel mentions two groups of people: those who call on the Lord's name and those whom the Lord calls. The ability to call on the name of the Lord comes only because of God's initiative in pouring out his Spirit. God's gracious love is demonstrated in his continuous call to his people. In the postexilic interpretation of OT history, God is described as the one who gives his good Spirit to teach his people (Neh 9:20). Similarly, when the Lord warns them through his prophets, it is by his Spirit (Neh 9:30). The Spirit plays a vital role in instructing the people so that they might understand. In the NT, it is the Spirit who enables people to confess Jesus as Lord (1 Cor 12:3) and empowers them to be witnesses for Christ (Acts 1:8; 2:4).

The promise of the Holy Spirit is not just for the Israelites; it is also for the Gentiles. In his Pentecost sermon, Peter is inclusive in his interpretation of the fulfillment of Joel's prophecy (Acts 2:17–21). The outpouring of the Spirit is now extended to all nations, near and far (Acts 2:38–39), and includes those of any age, gender, or social class. In recent years, the inclusive work of the Holy Spirit has been seen in spectacular ways in many parts of Asia and Africa. There are well-documented reports of men and women in the Islamic world – who have had no knowledge of the gospel and no contact with Christians in their community – experiencing dreams and visions of Jesus Christ. Many report seeing a figure of a man in white clothing they identify as Jesus; some have heard him speaking words from the Scripture to them, words they had never heard before, while others say that Jesus told them to do something; and many of these men and women say that their dream or vision led to a feeling of being clean or at peace.[2]

Joel's prophecy about the Spirit being poured out upon God's people was first realized at Pentecost. And the same Holy Spirit continues to fill his people, dwelling within them and among them, and directing and equipping them for evangelism and ministry.

3:1–21 THE RESTORATION OF GOD'S PEOPLE

In the first part of the book (1:1–2:17), Joel used the devastation caused by the locust plague to warn God's people to repent and invite them to return to him. The second part of the book (2:18–3:21) describes God's response to his people's repentance. Joel's message of hope began with the declaration, "Then the LORD was jealous for his land and took pity on his people" (2:18), then went on to describe both the material and spiritual blessings the Lord would shower on his people (2:19–32). Joel 3:1–21 deals with the final day of the Lord and the restoration of God's people. Of the eighteen explicit references to "the day of the LORD" in the OT, five are found in this short book (1:15; 2:1, 11, 31; 3:14). Joel defines the final day of the Lord as the decisive moment of judgment against God's enemies as well as vindication for God's people (3:1, 20). This final section has three parts: (a) God's judgment (3:1–8), (b) God's victory (3:9–16), and (c) God's blessing (3:17–21).

3:1–8 God's Judgment

In fulfilling his promise of restoration God will judge the nations for what they did to his people. This section pertaining to God's judgment has three parts: (a) the case against the nations (3:1–2a), (b) the charges against the nations (3:2b–6), and (c) the consequences for the nations (3:7–8).

---

2. Darren Carlson, "When Muslims Dream of Jesus." See https://www.thegospelcoalition.org/article/muslims-dream-jesus/, accessed September 30, 2020.

The Case against the Nations

Having described the signs that would herald the day of the Lord (2:30–31), the prophet now announces what will occur on that day. This will be a time when God restores the fortunes of his people (3:1; compare Jer 33:10–16) and pronounces judgment on the nations for what they have done to God's land and his people (3:2; compare Zeph 3:8). Israel is God's inheritance, and the repeated "my people" (3:2–3) emphasizes this special relationship between Israel and the Lord (Deut 9:26, 29).

The case will be taken up at the Valley of Jehoshaphat. This term only occurs in Joel (3:2, 12) and means "the valley of judgment of the Lord." It may refer to a specific place, which is associated with the seriousness of the crimes committed, or be a symbolic reference to the final judgment.[3] The reference to "Jehoshaphat" may allude to a previous judgment of God against Judah's enemies in the time of King Jehoshaphat (2 Chr 20:1–30) and thereby serve as a reminder of God's future judgment.

The Charges against the Nations

In the Lord's case against the nations, specific reference is made to Tyre, Sidon, Philistia, Egypt, and Edom (3:4, 19). The first charge against the nations is that they have the scattered God's people among the nations (3:2). This may refer to the Babylonian deportation of Judah in 586 BC. In this deportation, the people of Judah were scattered, provoking taunts by the nations (2:17, 19).

Second, the enemies have divided up the land (3:2). In Israel, the land was a gift from God, part of the blessing promised to Abraham and his descendants (Gen 15:7–8; 17:8; 28:4). God was the owner of the land, and the people of God held it in trust (Lev 25:23). Joshua distributed the land among the different tribes (Josh 13:7). When enemies divide up the land, it is in defiance against the owner and giver of the land (Joel 3:2).

Third, the nations are selling God's people by casting lots (3:3). In the OT, casting lots was sometimes used to make decisions or to determine God's will (Lev 16:8). In this context, however, the term is used negatively in the sense of selling people by random choice based on how the lot fell. Just as wicked nations sold people in Joel's day, in Asia today, evil people steal and sell women and children into sexual slavery. Sex is God's gift to married couples (Prov 5:15–19); rape, sexual abuse, prostitution, pornography, marital rape, and

---

3. In Isaiah, the judgment day is in the Valley of vision (Isa 22:5). Just like Joel, it is not a day of deliverance, but a day of destruction and terror.

sexual slavery show disdain for this gift and dishonor its giver. Children are a blessing from God (Ps 127:3); those who barter boys and girls, making them tradable commodities, demonstrate how little they value God's precious gift of children. Sex trafficking is tantamount to slave trafficking since victims are powerless to free themselves from their oppressors. Christians cannot simply ignore these facts or refuse to take action. Since we are all created in God's image and likeness, every human life is precious. Sex trafficking reflects the depravity of human beings in a fallen world; but as Christ's followers, we are called to protect the sanctity of life and marriage.

Joel then brings specific charges against the Phoenicians (Tyre and Sidon) and Philistines (Philistia) for their crimes (3:4). Tyre and Sidon were Israel's northern neighbors, while the region of Philistia lay southwest of Israel. Both groups were traditional enemies of Israel. Tyre was "the marketplace of the nations" (Isa 23:3) and, along with Sidon, a port city and prominent commercial center (Ezek 27:1–9). Both Phoenicians and Philistines were slave traders (Amos 1:6, 9). There are two specific indictments against Tyre, Sidon, and Philistia. First, they have looted the temple treasury and taken God's treasures to their own pagan temples (3:5). Second, they have sold God's people as slaves to the Greeks, known for slave trading (3:6).[4] These are crimes against God (3:5) and they will face retribution (3:4, 7).

The Consequences for the Nations

In consequence of God's judgment the people of Tyre, Sidon, and Philistia will experience shame (3:7–8). Their worldwide trade in abundant goods will come to an end and their sons and daughters become commodities. God, as the merchant, would allow them to be sold as slaves to "a nation far away." That nation was Sheba, in Arabia – one of Tyre's former trading partners and a rich nation that was involved in slave trading (Ezek 37:22–23). In this way, they would understand the evils of enslaving the people of Israel. Once they were slave-traders, now they themselves will become slaves.

---

4. Baker, *Joel, Obadiah, Malachi*, 105.

RAISING OUR VOICES TO
PROTECT THE VULNERABLE

Joel describes the depths of sin to which the nations have sunk: "They cast lots for my people and traded boys for prostitutes; they sold girls for wine to drink" (3:3). But what Joel describes is not just some long-ago scandal. Even today, in parts of Asia, such evils continue. Human traffickers and slave-owners buy women and children, transport them across borders to other countries, and sell them for sex slavery or bonded labor.

Dan Brown, author of *Inferno*, writes, "Manila had six-hour traffic jams, suffocating pollution (and) a horrifying sex trade, whose workers consisted primarily of young children."[1] He even describes the Philippines as the "gates of hell." The "Sex-for-Fly" probe in the Philippines revealed that when Overseas Filipino Workers (OFWs) – who were being raped, physically abused, or whose salaries were being withheld by their employers – appealed to government representatives overseas for help to return home, they were asked to perform sexual favors to raise money for their plane tickets home.[2]

All people, both male and female, are created in the image of God (Gen 1:26–27). This invests each person – whether man, woman, or child – with tremendous dignity. The Law and the Prophets insist on the need to love everyone in the community and to extend special care to vulnerable groups – widows, orphans, strangers, and the poor. As God's people, we dare not close our eyes and ears to the horror stories being lived out around us. First, we must lift our voices to God, asking that his justice prevail. Second, we must raise our voices on behalf of the voiceless and join the fight for justice for those who are vulnerable.

---

1. Cited in Dan Brown, *The arrogant opportunist*. Manila Bulletin, 2 June 2013. See https://ph.news.yahoo.com/dan-brown-arrogant-opportunist-171918024 .html, accessed on March 23, 2021.
2. Mario B. Casayuran, "3 'Sex-For-Fly' Victims Get Assistance," Manila Bulletin, Vol. 486, No. 27 (June 27, 2013), 6.

3:9–17 God's Victory

This section begins with a call to execute God's judgment. Whereas previous oracles addressed the Israelites (1:14; 2:15), this proclamation is made to the nations. God warns the nations to get ready for a skirmish (3:9–12) and a sentencing (3:13–17). The Valley of Jehoshaphat is the place of judgment for the nations (3:12). For Israel, however, this "valley of decision" (3:14) will be their vindication.

Who is entrusted with the task of proclaiming God's message to the nations (3:9a)? One suggestion is that an unnamed messenger is tasked with relaying the message to the nations. The command to "prepare for war" and "rouse the warriors" (3:9b) is a call to face the challenges of conflict (3:9–12) and indictment (3:13–17).[5]

A second suggestion is that the warriors of Judah are being enlisted to fight a holy war against the nations. They are to turn from their peaceful life to fight against God's enemies (3:10). At the valley of decision, they are to execute God's judgment against his enemies (3:13).[6]

The authors favor the first interpretation. God, through his prophet Joel, is summoning the nations to prepare for a skirmish (3:9–12). To prepare (literally, "sanctify") for war recalls the earlier calls to declare a holy fast (1:14; 2:15). This is a holy war. The nations will come with their warriors to do battle against the Almighty God.

The agricultural tools of plowshares and pruning hooks are used in the cultivation and harvesting of grapes. Plowshares are used for digging in the hill country. Pruning hooks are used to maximize the production of vines. Swords and spears are tactical weapons in ancient warfare.[7] The nations are to beat their plowshares into swords and their pruning hooks into spears (3:10). This is a reversal of the promise of peace in Isaiah 2:4 and Micah 4:3. This is because Joel is describing the time of conflict and judgment that will precede the experience of blessing in God's kingdom.

The wicked nations will have to face God the warrior. No one is exempt. Not just the warriors and the fighting men, but even the "weakling" must come to do battle. Not only must the nations assemble, they must "come

---

5. Hubbard, *Joel and Amos*, 84; Crenshaw, *Joel*, 187.
6. Barton, *Joel and Obadiah*, 103.
7. Seung Ho Bang, "For Whom the Plowshares and Pruning Toil: A Tradition-Historical Reading of Joel 4.10," *JSOT* 39 (2015): 505–512.

quickly" (3:11a). The three verbs – come, assemble, bring down – emphasize both certainty and the sense of urgency. They will face the real warrior – God!

The Lord is asked to bring his warriors to fight (3:11b). These are God's heavenly armies (compare Josh 5:13–15). Everyone must come to the Valley of Jehoshaphat, where the Lord will judge all nations. The call to war is a call to judgment. The Valley of Jehoshaphat is the valley of decision (3:12, 14)!

The nations must prepare for sentencing (3:13–17). The Lord's judgment is described using images drawn from agriculture. As in other parts of the Bible, the harvest is used as a metaphor for judgment (Isa 17:4–6; 63:1–6). The grain is ready for harvesting. The winepress is so full of grapes for treading that the vats overflow. The harvest seems impressive, recalling the prosperity depicted in Joel 2:24 – "the threshing floors will be filled with grain; the vats will overflow with new wine and oil" – except that this is a harvest of wickedness. That the harvest is "ripe" signifies that the time is ripe for God's judgment. The command to the Lord's own warriors to "swing the sickle" represents execution of God's judgment (3:13; compare Rev 14:14–20).

As the multitudes gather at the Valley of Jehoshaphat (3:12), it is decision time. The repetition of "valley of decision" (3:14) emphasizes the certainty of the Lord's indictment against the nations. The nations decided to rebel against him; now it is his turn to decide against them and he will punish them for their great wickedness (3:13). The nearness of the day of the Lord means that this destruction is at hand. The valley of decision is the valley of judgment.

The day of the Lord is the last day (the eschatological day). It evokes a cosmic catastrophe in that dreadful day (3:15; compare 2:10, 31). God created the sun, moon, and stars. But he will also darken them at the right moment as signs of the day of the Lord (Matt 24:29).

The image of the Lord roaring from Zion and thundering from Jerusalem is directly related to the day of the Lord (3:16a; Amos 1:2). It signals impending judgment against his enemies. God's judgment is compared to a lion's attack (Isa 38:13). The roar of the lion comes after the beast has caught its prey (Amos 3:4, 8), it is a sound of victory after punishment (Hos 5:14). These are the images of the lion-king who is the enemy of evil and who will roar as a symbol of victory. The Lord roars against the nations that are his enemies (Jer 25:30–31); at his roar, the heavens shake with fear and the earth quakes (3:16a; compare Isa 29:6). But for God's people, the children of Israel, the Lord's roar is reassuring, reminding them that he is their refuge and stronghold (3:16b; Ps 27:1; Isa 25:4; Jer 17:17).

Amid judgment for the nations, the people of God experience his blessings and protection and recognize that God is in their midst. This recognition of God in their midst is an important theological theme in Joel (3:17; see 2:27). The living God promises to dwell in the midst of his people. This gift of God's presence was already promised in the Law for those who keep God's covenant (Lev 26:11–13) and it will ensure enduring peace and protection for them (1 Kgs 6:13). The Israelites first experienced this in the wilderness, where the tabernacle was God's dwelling place (Exod 25:8). The reference to Zion, God's holy hill, is not just symbolic but goes back to David's desire to build a house for the Lord (2 Sam 7:1–16). It was God's presence that made Jerusalem the holy city (compare Isa 52:1; Zech 14:21). Now, once again, God will dwell with his people on the holy hill, in Jerusalem (Joel 3:17). There will be no more shameful invasions, no more foreign influence. Henceforth the people will be able to worship the Lord as their one true God.

The promise of God for his people is his very presence which strengthens them to face any challenge that comes their way. The difference between those who believe in God and those who do not is the experience of God's peace even in the midst of storms.

God is a refuge and a stronghold for his people (3:16). God's judgment will destroy his enemies and his redemption will bring salvation for his people, among whom he shall dwell forever.

3:18–21 God's Blessing

This final section of Joel's message points to the eschatological hope – what God will do for his people in the future (compare 3:1). He will demonstrate his care through the blessings of his presence and his presents (3:18–21). Instead of shameful devastation, the people of God now enjoy life in God's presence. In contrast to the earlier situation – where there was no new wine because of calamity (1:5), no milk from the cattle because the pasturelands had dried up (1:18), and no water because of drought (1:11–12) – God's people now enjoy an abundance of new wine, milk, and water (3:18; compare Isa 55:1–3). They will have new wine for social gatherings, milk for food, and water that was crucial for survival. The mountains once full of enemy soldiers (2:1–2, 5) will "drip new wine" and "flow with milk" (3:18). The blessing of dripping wine emphasizes the abundance and restoration of that day (compare Amos 9:13). The fountain that will flow out of the Lord's house signifies continuous blessings; flowing water from the temple is a prophetic promise for the future (compare Ezek 47:1–12; Rev 22:1–2), pointing to transformation and renewal.

The purpose of the fountain is to water the "valley of acacias" (or "Valley of Shittim"). Acacia wood was used for making the altar of incense in the tabernacle (Exod 30:1–2). The identity of the Valley of Shittim is unknown. Whether this fountain is intended to water the acacia tree or the Valley of Shittim, its main purpose is to bless the people who live there.

God's blessings on his people include the punishment of their enemies which results in their own vindication (3:19–21a). The neighboring nations Egypt and Edom were ancient enemies of the people of God. Egypt's antagonism, which had begun during Israel's years of bondage and the exodus event, had continued over the years. Edom had been vicious in its treatment of God's people during the fall of Judah and Jerusalem in 586 BC (Obad 10–14). Both countries would be laid to waste.

Joel's concluding word is about the dwelling of God (3:21b). It is a blessing for the covenant people to follow him and receive this blessing (compare Lev 26:11–12).

The postexilic prophet Joel presents the sovereign Lord as the God of his people – no other god is equal to him. Like other postexilic prophets, Joel directs the priests to call a sacred assembly in Zion and fast and pray for the restoration of the people. In the first part of the book, Joel focuses on the theme of destruction – a warning to the people. In the second, he focuses on the theme of restoration – a promise for God's people. Using the vivid imagery of locusts and armies, the prophet challenges the people to renew their commitment to God. The Lord himself summons his people to come to him before the coming of the day of the Lord. He is gracious and compassionate, but he is also just and will judge the wicked. The Lord is present with his people by his Spirit, who will be poured out on all who call on God's name. His promise of presence gives us eternal hope! Truly, the Lord is God!

FAITH AMID COVID-19 FEARS

These days of our lives under COVID-19 scare,
With global virus looming around no one is spare,
In times like this, we look up to our Lord Jesus –
"Peace be with you," He says, proving He always cares.

Chorus:
    COVID-19, come what may!
    Jesus has conquered all the way;
    Despite this boundless pandemic,
    We rest assured in Him each day.

Our frontliners – doctors, nurses, and all ground workers,
Stay tirelessly attending the sick and those weaker;
We pray, our Lord Jesus, be their personal Savior
"Come, those who are weary," He says to all seekers.

The earth will soon be wrapped up like an old cloth,
Everything we hold so dear will disappear like froth;
The New Heaven and Earth to come with Jesus as King,
"Take heart, I've overcome," His words, true worth!

Rosa Shao

THE BOOK OF NAHUM

INTRODUCTION

AUTHORSHIP AND DATE

Nahum lived during the time of the Assyrian Empire and prophesied about the fall of its capital city, Nineveh. He was from Elkosh, a small town in Judah. Although its specific location is unknown, some scholars have suggested that this town was Capernaum (meaning "village of Nahum"). The prophet's name means "comfort": "The root has a meaning 'be relieved by taking vengeance' (Isa 1:24; 57:6), and this would be especially fitting for Nahum. Comfort and relief are brought to God's people when he takes vengeance on their enemies!"[1]

Though no date is mentioned in the text, two important events provide a timeframe for the delivery of Nahum's message. The first is the fall of Thebes (3:8), sometimes translated as, "No-amon" (NASB). This took place in 663 BC, during the time of Ashurbanipal. The second event is the fall of Nineveh, the capital of Assyria (2:8; 3:7). Nineveh fell to the Babylonians and Medes in 612 BC, under the leadership of Nabopolassar, after a three-month siege against Nineveh. Thus, Nahum would have prophesied between 663 BC and 612 BC.

HISTORICAL CONTEXT

In the seventh century BC, Nineveh replaced Assur as the capital of the Assyrian Empire and was famed as a powerful fortified city. Assyria had a long history of oppression against Judah and other nations. In their pursuit of power and expansion, the Assyrians committed many atrocities, hurting and displacing people. Eighth-century prophets like Isaiah and Micah asserted that Assyria was God's instrument of judgment against his chosen people. But this gave rise to questions about God's justice: Why would God use an evil empire against his people and spare it the punishment of his wrath?

Beginning in the latter half of the eighth century, the Assyrians expanded their empire, dominating the Near East for over a century under the rule of kings such as Tiglath-Pileser III, Shalmaneser V, Sargon II, Sennacherib, and Esarhaddon. But it was during the reign of Ashurbanipal that Assyria was at its greatest, both in terms of political power and cultural achievements. In 663 BC, Ashurbanipal even conquered Thebes, the ancient capital

---

1. G. M. Butterworth, "Nahum," in NBC, 21st century edition, 4th edition, eds. D. A. Carson et al. (Leicester, UK: Inter-Varsity Press, 1994), 834.

of Egypt. Instability and rebellion, however, characterized the latter part of Ashurbanipal's reign. His death in 627 BC coincided with the rise of serious threats to Assyria. Ashurbanipal's sons who succeeded him were weak kings. As such, Cyaxares, king of the Medes, secured control of Persia and moved westward, besieging Nineveh in 625 BC even though he failed to conquer it. In the south, Nabopolassar revolted against Assyria, becoming king of Babylon in 625 BC. Thereafter, the Babylonians, Medes, and Scythians formed an alliance to overthrow Assyria. The fall of Nineveh in 612 BC marked the end of the great Assyrian Empire.

AN ASIAN THEOLOGICAL READING OF NAHUM

As part of God's revealed word, the book of Nahum gives us principles applicable in any culture. But two themes are of particular relevance for Asian readers.

The Lord's Honor and People's Honor

In Asian culture, honor is significant. Further, it is associated with hierarchy. The person at the topmost level of the hierarchy receives the most honor and respect. The eldest member in the family is regarded as its head. One of his key functions is to act swiftly to defend the honor and reputation of the family whenever the need to do so arises.

In the book of Nahum, God, the highest person in the family of Israel, comes to the defense of Israel. He defends Israel's honor by defeating their enemies (1:2).[2] In the process, he also defends his majesty and character (1:2–8). As such, the enemies' plot against the people is portrayed as a plot against the Lord (1:9). Their wickedness is seen as being against God (1:11). Hence, the Lord is against them (3:5–7). As the Lord restores his own honor, the people's honor is restored. That is the primary role of the person at the topmost level in the family hierarchy. And the Lord is faithful to that task.

The Oppressor and the Oppressed

Many Asian countries were once colonized by powerful Western nations. As early as the twelfth century, countries east of Europe were categorized as Near East, Middle East, and Far East, on the assumption that Europe was the center of the world. From the perspective of sixteenth-century colonizers such as Portugal and Spain who set out on voyages of discovery and conquest, a

---

2. Gregory Cook, "Nahum Prophetic Name," *TynBul* 67 (2016): 37–40.

country such as the Philippines lay the farthest away from their native Europe.[3] But this geopolitical term, "Far East," also implied that the Western countries have more developed cultures than the countries in Asia. Today, the offensive label "Far East" is no longer used; instead, "Asia" is used as a general term for this region.

Nahum's prophecy is a comfort to the victims and a warning to the oppressors. The Lord is a refuge in times of trouble for those who trust in him (1:7). But this does not mean that human oppression ceases. Even now, to families in Asia – who are displaced through war or human sins such as sex trafficking – it may seem that God is silent. But through those who fight for justice, God brings comfort to those who are suffering and, sometimes, deliverance.

Ultimately, however, God's wrath will discipline nations and people who have oppressed others. He is against wickedness and sins, and he will judge inhumane oppression. Nahum testifies to this. When Nineveh besieges a country, there is bloodshed and plundering (3:1). Women and children are disgraced and sold into slavery (3:4–5, 10, 19). Endless cruelty and captives are part of the results of war (3:10, 19). Nineveh is judged because of its atrocities and abuse of power. When the Lord judges one party, this means deliverance for the other party.

God's judgment against Babylon for its oppression of Israel serves as a warning to us. We must be careful how we live, both as individuals and as citizens of nations and of the global village. The book of Nahum challenges us to act justly and to uphold justice.

THEOLOGICAL THEMES

The message of the book is one of hope to nations and peoples who were oppressed. The central event is the fall of a great nation because of the judgment of God. The Lord is the divine warrior who cares for his people and exercises justice. God's righteousness and goodness demand this justice.

God's Righteousness

God demonstrates his righteousness by judging evil (1:2–3). As the Creator, God displays his mighty power and his cosmic supremacy from the heavens to

---

3. For a comparison of how the oppressed felt with the book of Revelation, see Samson L. Uytanlet, "The Sound of Silence: A Literary Comparison between Jose Rizal's *Noli Me Tangere* and John of Patmos' *Revelation of Jesus*," in *Scripture and Service: A Celebration of Life, Essays in Honor of Joseph Shao*, ed. Samson L. Uytanlet (Valenzuela City: Biblical Seminary of the Philippines, 2019), 133–160.

the earth, from sea to mountains (1:4–5). He is the avenger of cruelty, idolatry, and immorality. As the jealous God, he takes vengeance against the enemies of his people. The Assyrians are ruthless and arrogant, but God will judge them. The Lord is against them because of their mistreatment of his people and other nations (2:13; 3:5). The "city of blood" will have to be destroyed (3:1). God's action results in the triumph of justice (1:3–8; 2:3–13; 3:1–19).

God's Goodness

The deliverance of his people is guaranteed! God's goodness will guarantee it. In the midst of threats from their enemies, there are always promises for God's people (1:12–13). The Lord, as the warrior who fights for his people, will restore their splendor (2:2). In times of trouble, the Lord is a refuge. Those who trust in him experience his care for them (1:7). He liberates his people from their affliction (1:8, 12). Peace is proclaimed with the divine punishment of Nineveh (1:15). Divine justice brings a message of hope. God brings comforts to his oppressed people. For the despondent, destitute, and hopeless, he offers hope (2:2). The cruelty of the oppressor will be eliminated (2:13; 3:19). The Lord will restore the splendor of his people (2:2; compare Isa 40:1–2). By bringing down the powerful, he lifts up the lowly. He is always good to those who take refuge in him.

UNITY

The message of Nahum, beginning with a hymn (1:2–8) and closing with a funeral dirge (3:18–19), presents a clear message of judgment against Nineveh. A decree is proclaimed (1:9–15), and it will assuredly be implemented (2:1–3:19).

Nineveh plots evil against the Lord, but he has foretold its destruction (1:11; 3:19). He declares his opposition to Nineveh and will take action against the city (2:13; 3:5–6). Judgment of Nineveh means salvation for Judah (1:12, 14–15; 2:1–2). Two motifs stand out in every chapter, both related to destruction: first, the imagery of annihilation by fire (1:10; 2:13; 3:13, 15); second, the imagery of the military catastrophe (1:14–15; 2:13; 3:2–3, 12–15).

Each chapter ends with a reference to some form of good news. Nahum 1 ends with a messenger of good news proclaiming peace to Judah (1:15). In Nahum 2, the voices of the Assyrian messengers will no longer be heard (2:13), and this is good news for Judah. Nahum 3 concludes with the statement that all who hear will rejoice over the news that Assyria has fallen (3:19).

USE OF TORAH AND PROPHETIC TRADITION

The assertions "the LORD is slow to anger" and "the LORD will not leave the guilty unpunished" (1:3) come from two great texts in the Torah/Law: Exodus 34:6–7 and Numbers 14:18–19. These statements, which emphasize both God's patience and his justice, are often repeated in the Writings (Pss 86:15; 103:8; 145:8) and in the Prophets (Joel 2:13; Jonah 4:2).

The book of Nahum begins and ends by describing Assyria's cruelty and arrogance: Assyria "plots evil" and "devises wicked plans" (1:11) and is guilty of "endless cruelty" (3:19). In this, Nahum stands in continuity with Isaiah and Zephaniah, who also denounce the wickedness of Assyria (Isa 10:5–9; Zeph 2:13–15). But Nahum also specifies that God is against the city of Nineveh because of its cruelty (2:13; 3:5).

NEW TESTAMENT CONNECTIONS

Nahum's declaration, "The feet of one who brings good news, who proclaims peace!" (1:15) resembles the messianic passage in Isaiah 52:7, which Paul cites in Romans 10:15: "How beautiful are the feet of those who bring good news!" The emphasis is on both the bearer of good news and the content of the message. The bearer must be bold enough to share the good news, and the message must be clear. In Nahum, the good news for Judah is that God will destroy the oppressor. The prophetic word about God's wrath and judgment restores hope for God's people. The good news of peace must be proclaimed so that people can appreciate God's magnificent salvation (1:15; Isa 52:10).

The balance between God's patience and his justice (1:3) finds an echo in Paul's reference to "the kindness and sternness of God" (Rom 11:22). According to Paul, God hopes that his kindness will lead them to repentance (Rom 2:4).

In addition to the above connections, there is a contrast as well. In Nahum, God's wrath is against a nation; in the NT, it is against sin and wickedness (Rom 1:18–20). Paul writes that when people persisted in their wickedness, "God gave them over" to their sinful ways (Rom 1:24–32). The cross was God's solution to the problem of sin, offering hope to the people of God by rescuing them from God's wrath. As Jesus dies on the cross, crying, "It is finished" (John 19:30), the wrath of God is satisfied!

OUTLINE

NAHUM 1:1–15

GOOD NEWS FOR JUDAH

Nahum's oracles are against Nineveh and about its fall. Assyria's great wickedness calls for divine judgment. The condemnation of Nineveh means consolation for Judah. God's wrath against Nineveh means deliverance for God's people. The book of Nahum has two main parts: the first focuses on good news for Judah (1:1–15), the second announces bad news for Nineveh (2:1–3:19).

This first part of the book contains a hymn describing God's unchanging character (1:2–8), followed by an announcement that God's wrath will be poured out on Nineveh because of its wickedness (1:9–15).

1:1–8 WRATH OF GOD

After a brief statement about the identity of the prophet and the subject of his prophecy (1:1), a hymn is used to describe different facets of God's character: his jealousy, anger, patience, justice, goodness, and care (1:2–8).

1:1 Title

The book of Nahum contains a "prophecy" (or "oracle" ESV) concerning Nineveh and records the "vision" given to the prophet Nahum. Oracle means "burden" or "utterance." God gives this prophecy for the prophet to proclaim to the people (compare Mal 1:1). "Vision" refers to something that a prophet sees, a revelation from God, and it is often linked with the introductory words of the prophetic books (Isa 1:1; Obad 1).

1:2–8 Hymn about God

This section takes the form of a hymn or psalm describing the character of God (1:2–8). Because of its long history of brutality against Judah, Nineveh deserves divine punishment. The hymn depicts God as being on the side of his people, against those who oppress them. It has three main sections, describing God's ways (1:2–3a), his wrath against the guilty (1:3b–6), and his watchfulness over his people (1:7–8).

1:2–3a God's Ways: His Character

The people of God suffered greatly under the oppressive Assyrian Empire. Nineveh, its capital, had a long history of violence and cruelty. God acts to avenge his people, executing his vengeance through the forces of nature.

The poem begins by describing the character of the Lord who is both judge and deliverer. Jealousy refers not only to God's intolerance of his people's unfaithfulness (Exod 20:4–5; Deut 6:15; Josh 24:19) but also to his total commitment to his people (Joel 2:18) and his passionate protection of them (Ezek 36:5–6). The Lord is also "zealous" for his name (Ezek 39:25) and for his covenant people. Such is his zeal that he is compelled to intervene on their behalf when they are oppressed by other nations (Deut 32:35, 43; 2 Kgs 19:31; Isa 26:11). But God is just; he also acts to avenge the sin of his own people (Lev 26:25).

The hymn has repeated references to the Lord's vengeance and wrath. This "vengeance" must be understood in the light of the hostility and brutality of the Assyrian armies. God's zeal for justice is the reason for the divine indictment. The imperial aggression of Assyria is a grave threat to Judah and other nations. The despised oppressor must be defeated. Another way to view this concept of vengeance is to see it as the redress of the Lord,[1] who acts with zeal to right wrongs and restore justice.

God's wrath results in punishment. The oft-repeated creedal statement about God being "slow to anger" is paired with an affirmation of God's power and his commitment to justice (1:3; compare Exod 34:6–7; Num 14:18–19; Neh 9:17). In many places in the Bible, such confessions of God's graciousness affirm his patience and compassion for his people (Pss 86:15; 103:8; Joel 2:13). But being slow to anger does not mean that God will not express his anger, only that he delays punishment. Both forgiving and punishing reflect God's character. Divine judgment reflects his intention and his action to bring about justice. Punishment does not contradict God's goodness but is appropriate in the context of God's covenant relationship with his people.[2] This was part of God's revelation to Moses.

While Jonah focuses on God's compassion and forgiveness (Jonah 4:2), Nahum links God's compassion with his justice – the Lord will judge the

---

1. Julia M. O'Brien, *Nahum* (London/New York: Sheffield Academic Press, 2002), 48. See also John Goldingay, *Old Testament Theology, Vol. 2: Israel Faith* (Downers Grove: IVP Academic, 2006), 779–780.
2. Patrick D. Miller, *The Way of the Lord: Essays on Old Testament Theology* (Grand Rapids: Eerdmans, 2004), 272–273.

oppressors and "will not leave the guilty unpunished" (1:3). The oppressed people of God can take comfort in knowing that their oppressors will be brought to justice by God. When Jonah preached, the people of Nineveh escaped punishment because they repented. But their repentance did not last. And so they will soon experience God's judgment.

1:3b–6 God's Wrath against the Guilty

The various aspects of God's anger may be expressed with reference to natural phenomena such as whirlwind, storm, clouds, dust, sea, rivers, mountains, hills, earth, or fire (1:3b–6). The great and powerful Creator exercises complete control over his creation and often uses nature as a means of executing judgment against his enemies.

But this does not mean that every natural disaster is a punishment from God. In recent years, Asia has experienced many natural disasters – earthquakes, volcanic eruptions, typhoons, and tsunamis – which have resulted in great destruction and suffering. But we must not attribute all such calamities to divine wrath against sin. Suffering remains an incomprehensible mystery. Creation is the free decision of the triune God and his gratuitous gift to us. God had created an ordered universe and he allows calamities to happen without his constant intervention.[3]

God's mighty power is evident in his control over the powerful forces of nature. Whirlwind and storm often symbolize God's judgment (1:3b; Ps 83:15; Isa 29:6). So great is his power that the clouds are like mere dust beneath his feet (Ps 18:9). Sea and rivers symbolize freshness and fruitfulness, and are life-giving sources of food and water for the people. But when God rebukes the sea and the rivers, they become parched land (1:4a; Ps 106:9); at his command, the waters of the Red Sea parted to make a way for God's people (Exod 14:21–22). In contrast to the impotent gods of the Assyrians, God had demonstrated his power over the forces of nature both during the exodus from Egypt and the conquest of Canaan (Exod 15:1–18; Judg 5:4–5; 2 Sam 22:8–16).

Bashan in Transjordan, Carmel in northern Israel, and Lebanon in northwest Israel were fertile and fruitful places, symbolizing stability and prosperity (Deut 32:14; Isa 2:13; Jer 46:18). All three places are also mentioned in the context of God's judgment (1:4b; Isa 33:9). Without rains, even the most

---

3. Vinoth Ramachandra, *Sarah's Laughter: Doubt, Tears, and Christian Hope* (Carlisle, Cumbria: Langham Global Library, 2020), 88–93.

beautiful and fertile lands become barren and dry. Even mountains and hills, symbolic of stability and firmness, quake and shake under God's power and the inhabitants of the earth tremble before his majesty (1:5). The Creator rules over air, sea, and land. His control over each of these spheres (1:3b–5) is also evident in the story of Jonah, where God sends a violent storm, provides a big fish from the sea, and makes a vine spring up on the earth (Jonah 1:4, 17; 4:6).

The writer then poses two rhetorical questions that can only be answered in the negative (1:6a). "Who can withstand his indignation?" No one can. "Who can endure his fierce anger?" No person on earth can withstand the sovereign God, who is Creator, controller, and consummator of this world.

In the Old Testament, wrath and fire were common expressions of God's judgment (Isa 30:27; Jer 7:20; Lam 4:11). In the book of Psalms, "rock" denotes God's protection (Ps 27:5; 61:2). But contrary to that stability and security, "rocks are shattered before him" (1:6). In this context of judgment, images of fire and rocks both illustrate God's fierce indignation.

Nahum follows the tradition of the prophets in his depiction of God's anger and wrath. Divine anger and wrath are really divine justice and righteousness. In the teaching of the Law, God's wrath and anger were intended to bring people back to him (Lev 26:14–46). There is a difference between human and divine anger.[4] Human anger often results in a loss of control (Prov 15:18; 19:19; 29:22). God's anger, which establishes righteousness, is intentional; it is the result of his decision and his determination to bring about justice in the midst of sinfulness (Ezek 5:13). God's wrath and anger signify his hatred of sin and his displeasure at the disobedience and wickedness of his people (Isa 5:25; 9:8–21; Jer 4:4–26), as well as that of other nations (Isa 13:1–9). God's wrath is now against Assyria, which had once been "the club of [his] wrath" (Isa 10:5). In Nahum, God is fighting on behalf of his people.

1:7–8 God's Watchfulness over His People

God's goodness and compassion towards his own people does not lessen his power to judge the wicked. He is the vindicator of those who trust in him (1:7) but also the destroyer of the wicked (1:8). He is watchful over his people but wrathful against his enemies.

The goodness of the Lord was part of the liturgical formula by which his people praised him (Pss 100:5; 106:1; 107:1; 118:1). And his goodness is good

---

4. Gary A. Herion, "Wrath of God," in AYBD, Vol. 6, ed. David Noel Freedman, et. al. (New York: Doubleday, 1992), 991.

news to those who are being oppressed by the Assyrians. Nahum makes two statements about God's goodness (1:7). First, he is a refuge, a "stronghold" in times of trouble (1:7a; Pss 27:1; 37:39). Second, he "cares for" and understands the deepest needs of his people who trust him (1:7b).

As for God's enemies, the images of flood and darkness portray their complete destruction (1:8). The overpowering flood waters produce waves that sweep everything away. Similarly, the blackness of darkness depicts Nineveh's fall into obscurity. The punishment is both severe and comprehensive.

The hymn (1:2–8) has two simple themes: condemnation for God's enemies and consolation for God's people. The guilty will be punished (1:3), and Nineveh will come to an end (1:8). But this jealous and avenging Lord is a refuge for those who trust him (1:7). Nahum serves as a sequel to the book of Jonah. In Jonah, punishment was averted because of the repentance of the Assyrians. But in Nahum, the wickedness of Nineveh will be avenged and the justice and righteousness of God will triumph. Just as the star of the book of Jonah was the Lord, the hero of the book of Nahum is the Lord.

1:9–15 WICKEDNESS OF NINEVEH

Nineveh is denounced for its wickedness, and God's judgment is pronounced. The destruction of Nineveh signifies deliverance for Judah. God's anger is directed towards his enemies and his grace is displayed to his people. Nineveh's evil plots against the Lord will fail (1:9a, 11), and God's plans will prevail (1:9b–10, 12a, 14, 15b). As for Judah, instead of affliction and oppression (1:12b–13), they will enjoy God's peace (1:15a).

1:9–11 Nineveh's Plots Will Fail

The Lord will pursue and defeat the Assyrian Empire (1:8) because their evil plotting is, ultimately, against him (1:9a, 11). His judgment is certain – "he will bring to an end" their plotting (1:9a). And his judgment against Nineveh will be so complete that they will not trouble his people "a second time" (1:9b).

Nahum offers progressive images of troubles leading to total destruction with phrases like, "Entangled among thorns," "drunk from their wine," and "consumed like dry stubble" (1:10). Thorns prick those who touch them and thorns are often destined for destruction (2 Sam 23:6–7); those in a drunken stupor are unable to think clearly (Joel 1:5); dry stubble is light and easily devoured by the flames (Isa 5:24; Obad 18).

Although tasked with being God's rod against just one nation, Assyria plundered and destroyed many nations (Isa 10:5–7), including Judah. Plotting evil against God's people is tantamount to sinning against God. What great comfort in knowing that God defends his people!

The Assyrian Empire was the embodiment of "wicked plans" (1:11).[5] The word for "wicked" is a combination of "without" (*beli*) and "worth" (*ya'al*), meaning "worthlessness." So Nahum is making a play on words: the Assyrians are devising "wicked plans," but these are worthless and will come to nothing.

1:12–15 God's Plans Will Prevail

The reign of God is expressed in the form of judgment against Nineveh and salvation for God's people. There will be destruction for Nineveh (1:12a) but deliverance for Judah (1:12b–13). Nineveh's religious activities will cease (1:14), but Judah's religious celebrations will commence (1:15).

God's wrath is not only against the crimes of the Assyrian Empire but also against its gods. A jealous God permits no rivals (1:2; Exod 20:1–6). True worship of the Lord requires that idol-gods be destroyed (1:14–15). In Jonah, everyone in Nineveh calls on the true God (Jonah 3:1–10). In Nahum, Nineveh and all its false gods will be destroyed.

Two pronouncements are made. The first addresses only Judah, and gives a general picture of Nineveh's destruction as well as a message of comfort for Judah (1:12–13). The second pronouncement addresses both Assyria and Judah, and consists of a more detailed description of the extinction of Assyria and the promise to Judah (1:14–15).

1:12–13 The First Pronouncement

The first pronouncement begins with a messenger formula, "This is what the LORD says," indicating that the Lord himself is uttering this message (1:12a). The prophet is God's messenger and the message contains two interrelated ideas: comfort for Judah and punishment for Nineveh, which are two sides of a single message.

First, although they are numerous and have powerful allies, the Assyrians will be destroyed (1:12a) because of their brutal oppression of God's people. This had happened earlier when Assyrian forces under Sennacherib were eradicated (2 Kgs 19:32–36), and it would happen again.

Second, Judah receives a message of comfort (1:12b–13). Assyria's dominion over Judah was God's doing. But although God had afflicted his people,

---

5. The Hebrew word *beliyya'al* ("without worth") is left untranslated in the NT Greek as "Belial" to refer to Christ's enemy (2 Cor 6:15).

he would do so no longer. He had permitted it in the past; now he pledges to stop it. The Lord, the divine warrior, is powerful enough to overthrow this mighty enemy of Judah.[6]

The Lord will give freedom to Judah. The yoke (normally placed around the neck) and shackles (placed around the ankles), symbols of slavery and imprisonment, were intended to limit freedom and symbolized submission to tyrannical powers. Israel and Judah had suffered greatly under the yoke of Assyria's cruelties and demand for tributes. But that slavery and oppression will come to an end. In the biblical worldview, everything is under God's control. The Assyrian forces had served as God's agent in afflicting Judah, but they will do so no longer (1:12b).

1:14–15 The Second Pronouncement

The second pronouncement addresses both Nineveh and Judah. Again, it is introduced with a messenger formula – "The LORD has given a command" – and is a dual message of punishment to Nineveh and comfort to Judah. For Nineveh, the Lord's decree concerns both the political sphere and religious activities. Politically, there will be no more descendants who bear their name, an utterly shameful consequence (compare Ps 109:13). Religiously, the Lord would destroy their carved images and idol-gods. The Assyrians had desecrated many temples of other nations and King Sennacherib had acted with arrogance toward God and the temple in Jerusalem (2 Kgs 19:9–12; Isa 36:18–20). Now it was Assyria's turn for punishment as the Lord destroyed their carved images and the idols in their temples. It is the end of a politically and religiously evil empire.

The second part of the decree is a message of peace for Judah. A herald runs to proclaim this good news (Isa 52:7; Rom 10:15) – like a messenger running from the scene of a battle to bring welcome news of victory to a waiting king and people (2 Sam 18:26). The overthrow of this oppressive empire is encouraging news for Judah. Destruction will be replaced with peace from the Lord, a peace that involves celebration and fulfillment of vows (1:15b), a peace that will be welcomed by those who had suffered so long under Assyria. Jerusalem was surrounded by mountains (Ps 125:2) and a mountain was an effective place from which to declare the good news. The herald will run to proclaim that God's plan has been accomplished and that Nineveh has fallen.

---

6. Julia M. O'Brien, "Nahum-Habakkuk-Zephaniah: Reading the 'Former Prophets' in the Persian Period," *Int* 61 (2007): 176.

This will mean freedom of worship for God's people for they will be able to celebrate their religious feasts and fulfill their vows in thanksgiving for what God has done for them.

Is this relief from their enemies temporary or permanent for Judah? In 612 BC, the people of Judah would see with their own eyes the siege of Nineveh as God used the Babylonians, the Medes, and the Scythians to dig Nineveh's grave (1:14b; Ezek 32:22–23). The prophecy of Nahum was thus fulfilled.

The message of comfort and judgment should be interpreted within the context of Nahum 1. It is a message of hope to the faithful who trust in the Lord. The Lord is a jealous and avenging God. Although slow to anger, he will take vengeance on those who oppress God's people (1:2). Just as the Lord removed the Assyrian Empire with its numerous allies (1:12), he will remove the enemies of his faithful people. As the just God removed the Assyrian gods from their temples (1:14), God will remove the superpowers and rebels. God is in control. When God engages in battle, it is good news for his people. Peace will be established. Celebrations will begin (1:15)!

The message of Nahum should also be interpreted eschatologically. In the light of such great suffering in our world, this message is good news that must be shouted out from every mountain top to the peoples of every nation. The Lord is good, and he is a refuge in times of trouble for those who place their trust in him (1:7).

Nineveh's plots will fail but God's plans will prevail! God's sentence of judgment for the wicked is good news of salvation for the righteous.

RIGHTEOUS ANGER

Nahum's frequent references to God's anger can confuse modern readers because the New Testament often includes "anger" in its lists of sins: "Get rid of all bitterness, rage and anger, brawling and slander, along with every form of malice" (Eph 4:31; see also Gal 5:20; Col 3:8). Human wrath tends to be ignited when a person's rights are infringed: When Esau realized that his brother Jacob had deceitfully obtained the blessing that rightfully belonged to Esau, he said to himself, "I will kill my brother Jacob" (Gen 27:41). Human wrath frequently leads to vengeance. When Shechem defiled Dinah, Jacob's daughter, her brothers Simeon and Levi were furious; they retaliated by tricking the Shechemite men into being circumcised and then – while the men were still in pain and helpless to defend themselves – they killed them (Gen 34).

An incident from the book of Numbers illustrates the difference between sinful human anger and God's righteous indignation (Num 20:1–13). While on their way to the promised land, the Israelites grumbled about the lack of water. God told Moses to take his staff, gather the people, and speak to the rock, which would then pour out water. But although Moses assembled the people, he did not speak to the rock; instead, he raised his arm and struck the rock twice in anger. God was not pleased. He declared, "Because you did not trust in me enough to honor me as holy in the sight of the Israelites, you will not bring this community into the land I give them" (Num 20:12). Moses's actions sprang from frustration and anger, but God's response was the result of righteous indignation.

The psalmist warns, "Be angry, and do not sin; ponder in your own hearts on your beds, and be silent" (Ps 4:4 ESV). Righteous anger – for instance, getting angry when we see someone mercilessly beating a little child – is not only acceptable but necessary. We *must* get angry and take appropriate action in such situations. Anger that leads to justice is righteous anger; anger that leads to meanness or revenge is unrighteous and sinful anger.

The NT warns against sinful anger. Jesus said, "I tell you that anyone who is angry with a brother or sister will be subject to judgment" (Matt 5:22). Paraphrasing Psalm 4:4, Paul said, "'In your anger do not sin': Do not let the sun go down while you are still angry" (Eph 4:26). He also wrote, "Do not take revenge, my dear friends, but leave room for God's wrath, for it is written: 'It is mine to avenge; I will repay,' says the Lord" (Rom 12:19). James writes, "Everyone should be quick to listen, slow to speak and slow to become angry, because human anger does not produce the righteousness that God desires" (Jas 1:19–20).[1] In contrast, God's anger is driven by his desire to right the wrongs and bring justice. Nahum warns that God will not leave the guilty unpunished (Nah 1:3).

Today, when we witness injustice in the form of ethnic cleansing, racial prejudice, or the oppression of smaller nations by superpowers, we should cry out to God to display his anger and justice. Although Assyria acted as though it had every right to oppress nations like Israel, the God of justice was watching. The message of Nahum is that God promises to right all wrongs, avenge all evil, and bring justice – in his time.

When anger threatens to overwhelm us and tempt us to sin, reading psalms of lament – such as Psalms 44, 60, 74, 80 – or meditating on Nahum 1:2–8 can help us to release our anger and frustration to our Lord. Just as God listened to his people's laments and the psalmists' prayers, he will hear us. "The LORD is good, a refuge in times of trouble. He cares for those who trust in him" (Nah 1:7).

---

1. For more analysis on these two verses, see Luke L. Cheung and Andrew Spurgeon, *James: A Pastoral and Contextual Commentary*, ABCS (Carlisle, Cumbria: Langham Global Library, 2018), 34–35.

NAHUM 2:1–3:19

BAD NEWS FOR NINEVEH

The collapse of Nineveh was decreed in part one of the book of Nahum (1:1–15). This was good news for Judah. The second part of the book describes the terrible things that will befall the great city of Nineveh (2:1–3:19). This is bad news for Nineveh. This second section begins by describing God's war against Nineveh (2:1–13) and concludes with the pronouncement of woes against Nineveh (3:1–19).

2:1–13 WAR AGAINST NINEVEH

This chapter describes the destruction of Nineveh and gives the reasons for God's punishment of the Assyrian Empire. The prophet's message begins with an oracle (2:1–10) and ends with a dirge or taunt song (2:11–13). This divine war against Nineveh is described in four sections: Nineveh is warned of an imminent attack (2:1–2); the city is attacked (2:3–5); it is plundered (2:6–10); and, finally, Nineveh is taunted (2:11–13).

2:1–2 Warned

The oracle opens with a strong warning to Nineveh to prepare for an imminent attack. It is ironic that Nineveh has to prepare for war. It was once the invincible invader but now it will be invaded. Its fortress seemed impenetrable, but now it cannot be defended. In former times, Nineveh was the aggressor, and other nations had to be watchful; now Nineveh must be watchful, brace itself, and marshal its forces. In Nahum 1, Nineveh's doom was declared; now the city is warned to prepare to defend itself against the coming onslaught.

The fall of Nineveh will destroy the predators of God's people. Hence the warning to Nineveh is a promise of restoration for Jacob (2:2). Jacob and Israel are sometimes used synonymously (Gen 32:28; Ps 105:23; Hos 12:12) but, in this context, Jacob refers to the Southern Kingdom of Judah, while Israel denotes the Northern Kingdom.[1] So this restoration is for the whole

---

1. Carl E. Armerding argued that after the destruction of Samaria, the southern prophets reclaimed "Jacob" and "Israel" (Isa 14:1–4). Carl E. Armerding, "Nahum," in EBC, Revised, Vol. 8 (Grand Rapids: Zondervan, 2008), 580. So the restoration of Judah is envisaged here.

nation. In the preexilic era, the hope of the remnant is the restoration of the whole nation of Israel.[2]

Since Jacob and Israel are objects of pride and delight in God's eyes (Isa 60:15), he promises to restore their former splendor (2:2). This splendor involves the land and its produce. The Assyrian attacks had laid waste the land. When there is war, agricultural produce such as grain, grapes, and olive oil are destroyed, which affects the social gatherings and religious celebrations of the people of God. Vines were common in Judah, and the Bible frequently uses a vine or a vineyard as a symbol of Israel (Isa 5:1–7; Jer 2:21; Ps 80:8–13; Hos 10:1) or of God's blessings on his people (Joel 2:22; Mic 4:4).

The restoration of the splendor of God's people is the reason for the impending attack on Nineveh. This restoration follows what has already been promised in Nahum 1 – that the Lord will be a refuge for his people (1:7), that he will rescue them from the shackles of slavery (1:12a–13), and that they will rejoice in his gospel of peace (1:15).

2:3–5 Attacked

The Assyrian warriors were among the best-equipped in the ancient world. They used chariots and cavalry, and carried bows and spears.[3] Now these mighty armies will come under attack. The Medes and Babylonians, who will advance against Nineveh, will use the same types of equipment and methods of assault. Their attack will be swift.[4] Despite being forewarned, Nineveh will not be able to defend itself. The prophet describes the power of the armies (2:3–4) and the defeat of Nineveh (2:5). Assyria, once the victor, will become the victim. The predator will become the prey!

The soldiers and warriors of the Medes and the Babylonians are vividly and colorfully portrayed (2:3–4).[5] They symbolize terror and toughness. Chariots

---

Contrary to Carl Armerding, John Goldingay and Pamela J. Sealise stated that "Jacob" referred to the northern kingdom, while "Israel" described the southern kingdom. For Goldingay and Sealise, Nahum's promise is for both the northern kingdom and the southern kingdom. John Goldingay and Pamela J. Sealise, *Minor Prophets II*, NIBC (Peabody, MA: Hendrickson, 2009), 33.

2. In 1 and 2 Chronicles, "all Israel" is commonly used.

3. The Assyrian war machine is the most efficient in ancient Mesopotamia. See Joshua J. Mark, "Assyrian Warfare," https://www.ancient.eu/Assyrian_Warfare/, accessed October 1, 2020.

4. Aron Pinker argues that for swiftness the Babylonians used cavalry instead of chariots in their initial attack against Nineveh. Aron Pinker, "Nineveh's Defensive Strategy and Nahum 2–3," *ZAW* 118 (2006): 620–621.

5. Ezekiel depicts the Assyrian forces wearing blue (Ezek 23:6) and red (Ezek 23:14).

have been the principal strength of the Assyrian army. But now flashing metal chariots will ride against them. The war will be speedy. The brandishing of weapons indicates that the armies are ready for the kill. In years earlier, the Babylonians brought cedars and cypress trees from Lebanon (Isa 37:24) and transplanted them in their land. Now, they will use those same trees as "cypress spears" in the battle against the Assyrians (2:3 ESV).[6] Nineveh's defenses are weak (2:5). Its elite troops will set out to fight against the invasion, but they will be defeated on their way to the battlefield and will fail to defend the city wall.

2:6–10 Plundered

The victor is now the victim. The plunder of Nineveh begins. The oracle began with a call to Nineveh to prepare itself for the upcoming siege (2:1). The river gates, the city's main barricades, will be breached (2:6); the plunderer of Judah (2:2) will be plundered; and Nineveh's boundless treasures will be carried off as spoils of war (2:9–10). The siege is described using five images.

First, the strongholds of the river gates and the palace will face destruction (2:6a). The river gates will be breached even though the fortress of Nineveh, with its intricate system of canals, was believed to be impenetrable. This is followed by the fall of the palace (2:6b).

Second, the Ninevites will be exiled as captives (2:7).[7] The decree of exile comes from the Lord. The Assyrians had carried away many captives from Israel; now their own people will be carried away into exile and their women will become slaves. The dove metaphor suggests the anxious trembling of a dove in difficulties (2:7; Hos 11:11), while moaning like a dove expresses the groaning and mourning of those who suffer (Isa 38:14; Ezek 7:16). The Assyrians will moan in anguish over the devastation of the city.

Third, the captured city will be drained of its resources (2:8a). A pool usually represented a reservoir (Eccl 2:6) and a good water supply was a precious resource, vital for a city to flourish. Nineveh was surrounded by water but, because of the siege, the water would drain away. The city will be drained of its resources – both its people and its produce. The captives will cry out in vain for a halt to this assault on their city (2:8b).

Fourth, at the victor's triumphant cry, Nineveh's riches will be stolen (2:9). Historically, the Assyrians were the plunderers, carrying away the silver and

---

6. Gregory Cook, "Nahum's Shaking Cypresses," *BBR* 26 (2016): 1–6.
7. For a different way of reading this verse, see Aron Pinker, "Descent of the goddess Ishtar to the Netherworld and Nahum II, 8," *VT* 55 (2005): 100.

gold of other nations; now they will be plundered and their treasures will be taken away.

Fifth, the plunder of the city will devastate its people (2:10). The city is "pillaged, plundered, stripped" (2:10a). The Hebrew verbs (*buqah, mebuqah, mebulaqah*) convey a progressive picture of Nineveh's devastation – as a result of which, "hearts melt, knees give way, bodies tremble, every face grows pale" (2:10b), which is a depiction of the increasing physical and psychological pain of its people.

2:11–13 Taunt Song

Nahum 2 concludes with a dirge, a taunt song against the Empire. The lion motif is used to describe Nineveh and its people, with the lion symbolizing the Assyrian Empire and Nineveh representing the lions' den.

In the OT, "lion" often symbolizes the aggressor or destroyer – either the nations God uses as instruments of his judgment against Israel (Isa 5:29; Jer 4:7; 50:17) or God himself (Hos 5:14). The lion motif is particularly apt here because, as often depicted in Assyrian art, Assyrian kings not only hunted lions but also compared themselves to mighty lions. But now the predator (2:12) will be the prey (2:13). The mighty hunter, who mercilessly attacked its prey, has fallen prey to God's devouring judgment.

The den is the lions' home. It is where the lion and lioness feed their cubs (2:11a), a place of comfort and security (2:11b). It is the place to which the lion brought its mangled prey (2:12). Assyria, the mighty hunter, had conquered many nations, and Nineveh was rich with the spoils of war. The taunt song mocks, "Where now is the lions' den" (2:11a)? The lair is laid waste, the den is destroyed.

The declaration that the Lord is against Nineveh is good news for Judah (2:13). The divine warrior fights on behalf of his people. He is the prime mover in the conflict against Nineveh. The war against Assyria is an expression of God's righteous indignation.

Nineveh's destruction is described in terms of four things that will no longer be there: chariots, young lions, prey, and messengers (2:13). Chariots represent the military power of the Assyrian armies, while "young lions" are their mighty warriors. With their chariots burnt up and their soldiers killed, Assyria will no longer have any power over Judah. Nineveh will be preyed upon and will no longer have any prey. Finally, the voices of their messengers will no longer be heard. Assyrian messengers typically announced the unwelcome news of war to the nations they oppressed. But not anymore! There will be no more messages of doom from Nineveh to the nations. Nahum 1 closed with God's messenger proclaiming the good news of peace to Judah (1:15). Nahum 2 concludes with the good news that there are no more Assyrian messengers to bring bad news to God's people (2:13)!

The Assyrian Empire, which was God's instrument of judgment against Judah, may have thought it had the final word on those it conquered. But God is sovereign over both his people and the nations. Although he uses events, people, and nations as his instruments of judgment, no one should attempt to "play God." These tools of God's judgment are subject to his strict scrutiny. When Nineveh is tried and pronounced guilty, God's sentence of destruction will be carried out by the Medes and the Babylonians. Yet, Nineveh's fall is not attributed to the superior power of its opponents but to God's might (2:13).

It is a common fact that "justice delayed is justice denied." In our fallen world, true justice is sometimes denied and often delayed. But when we suffer because of injustice, let us remember that the God who is committed to righteousness and justice (Ps 33:5) is against the oppressor (2:13). Let us place our hope in the Lord, trusting that he will defend his people (2:1–2) and destroy his enemies (2:3–13). The Lion of Judah roars!

3:1–19 WOE TO NINEVEH

The cry of "woe" resounds as the prophet Nahum concludes the sad story of Nineveh's demise. "Woe" is both a grievous and a fearsome cry. Oracles of woe are common in prophetic literature. They are pronounced against foreign nations (Isa 33:1; Hab 2:6–19) and also against Israel (Isa 5:8–23; Jer 23:1).

Nineveh's downfall has already been announced (2:1–13; Isa 10:5–27); a more detailed description is now given through two woe oracles and a concluding taunt song and dirge. The first woe oracle denounces Nineveh for its sins and depicts it as utterly disgraced (3:1–7); the second woe oracle compares it with Thebes on Nile to illustrate its total defeat and destruction (3:8–13). And the chapter ends with a taunt song directed at the fallen city (3:14–19).

3:1–7 Disgraced

The first woe oracle has two elements: the reasons for judgment of a once glorious kingdom (3:1–4) and a pronouncement of judgment against its cruelty that leaves other nations bewildered, as expressed in two rhetorical questions (3:5–7).

The opening line affirms the reason for God's judgment: Nineveh has been a bloodthirsty "city of blood" (3:1). They had invaded other nations, storming in on their chariots, piling up dead bodies with their flashing swords and glittering spears. Now, death and destruction in their own city would mirror how they had treated other nations (3:2–3). The predator, Assyria, is now the prey (compare 2:5–12). They will hear the same sounds of the machinery of war: the crack of whips, the clatter of wheels, and the sounds of galloping horses and jolting chariots (3:2). The results of battle will be grim: "piles of dead bodies without number" (3:3).

The prophet cites harlotry and sorcery as the reasons for Nineveh's judgment. The city is likened to a prostitute, driven by "wanton lust," and "alluring" and "enslaving" the nations by its "prostitution" and "witchcraft" (3:4).

In the OT, Israel's unfaithfulness to God was often portrayed using the metaphor of an adulterous wife who prostituted herself with the nations (Ezek 16:1–48; 23:1–49). In the political sphere, this was seen in Israel's readiness to make alliances with powerful nations – including Assyria (Ezek 16:28; 23:7) – instead of trusting in the Lord. This invariably resulted in the corruption of its worship, as God's people began worshiping the gods of these foreign nations.

Now, it is Nineveh that is portrayed as the harlot. "Wanton lust" refers to Assyria's insatiable greed for political power and the wealth of other nations, while "sorceries" and "witchcraft" – which were condemned by God (Deut 18:10) – may refer to occult practices employed in their warfare.

It is because of Nineveh's great wickedness that God declares, "I am against you" (3:5a; compare 2:13). The divine warrior will punish his foes (compare 1:2). The Lord, who "will not leave the guilty unpunished" (1:3), will punish Nineveh by public humiliation and shaming – the usual punishment in those times for unfaithfulness or prostitution.

"I will lift your skirts over your face" implies uncovering what was once covered (Ezek 16:37), thereby publicly exposing "nakedness," which brings "shame" (3:5b; Jer 13:26). In Asian culture, to be publicly shamed is not merely degrading but destroys a person's status in society. "Pelt you with filth," "treat you with contempt," and "make you a spectacle" (3:6) emphasize that Assyria will be utterly and publicly disgraced before the nations whom it once oppressed and humiliated. The same nations that once admired Nineveh and wanted to trade with it will now flee, saying, "Nineveh is in ruins" (3:7a). Worse, there will be no one to mourn for or comfort Nineveh (3:7b). The city will be ruined and utterly despised.

3:8–13 Defeated

This second oracle points to the defeat of the mighty city Thebes (3:8–10) to show that Nineveh will fare no better (3:11–13). Assyria's vulnerability is described using three images: a frightened drunkard (3:11), a fig tree ripe for plucking (3:12), and a weakling who leaves the gates unguarded (3:13).

Thebes on the shores of the Nile in Upper Egypt was a great and glorious city, the capital of the Egyptian Empire. It served as a natural defense for the city (3:8) and enjoyed the support of the neighboring kingdoms of Cush in the South, Put in the East, and Libya in the West (3:9). Yet, despite its glory and might, despite its strong defenses and powerful allies, Thebes fell to the Assyrian king Ashurbanipal in 663 BC and great atrocities were committed against its people (3:10). A shameful end for a city famed for its splendor and supremacy! Nineveh is in no way better than Thebes (3:8) and its plight will be even worse (3:11–13).

Three images are used to describe Nineveh's plight. The first image speaks of drunkenness (3:11), recalling the earlier reference to "drunk with wine" which speaks of God's wrath and judgment (1:10). Nineveh will flee in fear, desperately seeking refuge.

The second image compares Nineveh's strong fortresses to fig trees where the fruit was ripe and ready for plucking (3:12). By just shaking the tree the fruit will fall right into the mouth of the eater; Nineveh is similarly vulnerable. Just as ripe figs are eaten, Nineveh will soon be consumed.

In the final image, Assyria's troops are ridiculed as "weaklings" (3:13a; Isa 19:16) who are untrained for war and cannot fight against their enemies. Instead of guarding the gate, they will flee. Without resistance, the city gates will not withstand enemy attacks (3:13b; compare 1:10; 2:6, 13).

3:14–19 Taunt Song

During the reign of Ashurbanipal, the Assyrian Empire reached its apex, both culturally and politically. But this mighty empire will soon become extinct. The final section of the book includes a taunt song (3:14–17) and a funeral dirge (3:18–19).

Water and walls are crucial for the defense of a city under siege. Although a series of commands – "draw," "strengthen," "work," "tread," and "repair" (3:14) – challenge Nineveh to prepare for a siege (3:14; compare 2:1), this is followed immediately by the statement that fire and sword will burn up or break down their defenses (3:15a). Nineveh is taunted about the futility of its preparations against an assault that will be like a locust invasion (3:15b; compare Joel 1:2–4; 2:2–11)! Even if they "multiply like locusts" (3:15c), they will still not be able to defend themselves.

The locust imagery is also used in connection with the city's prosperity (3:16) and security (3:17). As a center for trade, Nineveh had become wealthy through extensive trading with many merchants – so many that they are described as "more numerous than the stars in the sky" (3:16a; compare Gen 26:4). Like locusts who "strip the land," these merchants will strip the city of its wealth and flee (3:16b).

The city's guards and officials, who were responsible for the safety and welfare of the city, are also compared to the locusts because they are so numerous. But like the locusts who fly away when they feel the heat of the sun, when the city comes under attack these people will desert their posts, leaving the city without protection or leadership (3:17).

The concluding funeral dirge (3:18–19) addresses the "King of Assyria." This could be a reference to the god Ashur, the supreme god of the Assyrians, in which case Nahum is taunting not simply the demise of the Assyrian Empire but also the religion behind it.[8] "Shepherds" here could refer to royal or military leaders. The guards and officials responsible for the city's security and welfare have fled (3:17); its leaders are dead (3:18a). Just as sheep without a shepherd are hopelessly scattered, so the people are scattered with no leader to gather them and bring them back (3:18; compare Isa 13:14).

Nineveh's fall would be "fatal" – a wound for which no healing is possible (3:19a). Its fall would also be final – the city would never be rebuilt (for centuries, no one even knew where Nineveh lay buried; it was only in 1845 that archaeologists finally uncovered its ruins). This will mark the end of the Assyrian Empire. But bad news for Assyria will be good news for all who had suffered under its rule and experienced its "endless cruelty" (3:19b).

To the people of God, suffering for centuries under Assyrian oppression – and to all those who suffer injustice and oppression today – Nahum's words are reminders of timeless truths which comfort, strengthen, and instill hope. When the Assyrians oppress God's people, it is against the Lord himself that they plot evil (1:9–11); and this God is "a jealous and avenging God," who "vents his wrath on his enemies" (1:2). But, he is a refuge for those who trust in him (1:7). God promises to destroy the destroyer (2:13) and restore the splendor of his people (2:2). Because the Lord is against Assyria (2:13; 3:5), the victor will become the victim, the endless cruelty of the Assyrians *will* end (3:19).

---

8. Gregory D. Cook, "Of Gods and Kings: Ashur Imagery in Nahum," *BBR* 29 (2019): 9–31.

A CHRISTIAN PERSPECTIVE ON CALAMITIES

Calamities – earthquakes, flooding, hurricanes, tornadoes, volcanic eruptions, tsunamis, and storms – have multiplied across Asia. When disaster strikes, people often assume that God is angry with them and is seeking to destroy them. And anyone reading Nahum (1:2–8) will surely conclude that God *does* indeed use calamities as instruments of his judgment against human sin.

But are our perceptions accurate? Can all calamities be attributed to divine wrath? Do we perhaps fail to see how God spares the nations from total destruction? Even though regional disasters – like the floods in Thailand and the Philippines – are often devastating, they are not comparable to the almost total annihilation of animals and human beings in Noah's time. God has been faithful to his covenant with all creation, keeping his promise to Noah that "never again will the waters become a flood to destroy all life" (Gen 9:12–16). It is only because of God's love and faithfulness that humanity has been spared from total destruction.

Calamities are often reminders of human failure to be good stewards of the environment. God gave us a mandate: "Rule over the fish in the sea and the birds in the sky and over every living creature that moves on the ground" (Gen 1:28). David echoes this: "You made them rulers over the works of your hands; you put everything under their feet: all flocks and herds, and the animals of the wild, the birds in the sky, and the fish in the sea, all that swim the paths of the seas" (Ps 8:6–8). Unfortunately, even Christians sometime equate *rule* or dominion with domination and fail to understand that it is responsible stewardship. So instead of being caretakers of creation, we exploit the environment by irresponsible decisions and selfish actions – deforestation, slash and burn agriculture, allowing land erosion, building structures over waterways, overfishing, hunting animals to the point of extinction. These cause extensive and sometimes irreversible damage to the environment. It is easy to attribute such calamities to God and blame him for the resulting devastation and suffering. But calamities are not always God's chastisement; they are often the result of mismanagement of the earth by human beings.

Humanity's mandate to rule includes the responsibility to care for creation (Gen 2:15); and, as caretakers of creation, the Lord will require of us an account of our stewardship. So we must be intentional about preserving and protecting the environment. We are not to merely stop harming the environment but to actively care for it. And when innocent people suffer because of calamities, God's people must respond with compassion and practical action to alleviate suffering. Above all, we must pray for God's continued protection over our world and its people. The OT prophets frequently prayed for deliverance for God's people, even while they announced God's judgment. In a time of drought, Elijah prayed, "and the heavens gave rain, and the earth produced its crops" (Jas 5:18). As prophets of our time, we are called not only to proclaim God's justice but also to pray for his mercy and deliverance.

THE BOOK OF MALACHI

INTRODUCTION

AUTHORSHIP AND DATE

The identification of the author of Malachi is problematic since there is no mention of the prophet Malachi outside this book. The Septuagint (the Greek translation of the Old Testament) does not even have the proper name "Malachi." Instead, the root word *mal'ach* is translated "the messenger." In the book of Malachi, a priest is described as "the messenger of the LORD Almighty" (2:7), a messenger who would prepare the way for the Lord – who is described as "the messenger of the covenant" (3:1). So Malachi may either be a proper name or a title that means "my messenger" (since the "i" at the end signifies the possessive "my").

Since priests are offering sacrifices at the temple (1:7–10; 2:13; 3:8), it is likely that this book was written after the second temple was rebuilt in 515 BC. The use of the Akkadian loan word *peha* ("governor") may point to the period under Persian rule (1:8; Ezra 8:36; Neh 5:14) and the carelessness of the priests in carrying out their duties is in keeping with the situation during Nehemiah's absence from Jerusalem (2:1–2; Neh 13:4–11). Finally, the placement of the book of Malachi after Haggai and Zechariah denotes a postexilic timeframe.

HISTORICAL CONTEXT

The optimism of the Jewish exiles during the Persian period was sparked by the decree of Cyrus in 539 BC. As the exiles return, they begin rebuilding the temple. The postexilic setting of the book of Malachi reflects the conditions during the Persian period after the second temple has been rebuilt (1:10; 3:1, 10) and the sacrificial system and Levitical priesthood restored. The old political order of the monarchy is now a thing of the past, and the priests and Levites are once again the leaders of the community. The Jews who worship the Lord live in Jerusalem and Judah, a sub-province of the Persian Empire. The Jews who returned were mainly from Judah, the Southern Kingdom. During this period, Israel is used synonymously with Judah (2:11).

The lists of the three groups of returnees show that the returnees were not great in number (Ezra 2:1–70; 8:1–20; Neh 7:6–73). They had returned to their homeland with lofty messianic hopes and expectations of restoration. But they faced the hard realities of a nation in need of rebuilding. Their economic situation was difficult and a crisis of faith threatened the religious heritage of Israel. The Persian title of governor used here in Malachi, *peha*, is also used for Nehemiah the governor (1:8; Neh 5:14; 12:26). The prophet Malachi deals with the same basic issues faced by the returnees during the time of Nehemiah – they are disillusioned and they doubt God's love (1:2). Malachi addresses several issues that this returnee community faces.

First, the depravity of the priesthood in relation to both the sacrificial system and their responsibility to teach (1:6–2:9; compare Neh 13:4–9, 30), which necessitates addressing the role of the priests and the Levites in teaching the people and leading them to worship the Lord.

Second, the problem of mixed-faith marriages and divorce. The Jews had divorced their Israelite wives to marry non-Jewish women. By doing so, they were unfaithful to covenants with their fellow Israelites. Such marriages also led to unfaithfulness to God in the form of idolatry – for marriage to non-Jewish women often resulted in worship of their foreign gods (2:10–16; Ezra 9:1–2; 10:10–11; Neh 13:1–3, 23–27). It was vital that the community be committed to pursuing godly marital relationships.

Third, the importance of tithes and offerings to the Lord (3:8–10; Neh 10:32–39; 13:10–14). Giving is not just a custom to be observed but an opportunity for the people to respond to God's love. With right offerings, God's house will have enough "food." Nehemiah explains such offerings encourage the Levites to carry out their service to God in the temple (Neh 13:10–14).

Fourth, the social problem of exploitation within the community. Following the return from exile, working conditions in Jerusalem were unfavorable and the rich were getting richer while the poor were getting poorer (3:5; Neh 5:1–12).

Fifth, faithfulness to the Torah/Law is a dilemma for both priests and people (2:8–9; 4:4; Ezra 7:25–26; Neh 9:32–35; 13:15–22). The instructions in the Torah must be followed so that priests and people might know and obey the will of God.

AN ASIAN THEOLOGICAL READING

While God's word through his prophet Malachi is relevant to the global community, a few salient themes appeal particularly to Asian readers.

God as Witness and Restorer of Relationships

Asian societies place great value on harmonious relationships since such relationships produce peace and happiness. Among the Chinese, harmony is a significant traditional value. Chinese people are often reluctant to express discomfort and dissatisfaction, even when failure to express such emotions causes disharmony. In situations of conflict, intermediaries may help to promote harmony by facilitating communication between parties. These "go-betweens" listen to both parties and act as witnesses to what the parties have agreed upon. Their role is to avoid shame issues that may arise if problems are not properly resolved. An intermediary may sometimes serve as an adviser or counselor to both parties. Historically, matchmakers were tasked with linking up young people who would be likely to build a healthy and harmonious marriage. When a patriarch makes a last will, an executor is charged with ensuring that there is a smooth distribution of wealth to the next generation.

In Malachi, God acts as the "witness" in marital relationships (2:14). This is an important theological affirmation that our Lord is not only present during the exchanging of marriage vows but continues to be a witness to the couple's faithfulness in marriage. He rebukes husbands who are unfaithful to their wives. He draws husband and wife together in their relationship. He is present during conflicts and can help a couple to resolve disagreements. He is the defender who preserves and promotes enduring love in marriage.

Malachi announced that an intermediary like Elijah would be sent to turn the hearts of parents to their children and children to their parents (4:5–6). In authoritarian Asian families, this process must often begin with parents, particularly fathers, who exert considerable authority and influence over their children. God, the great restorer, makes such restoration possible, leading to harmonious relationships in families.

Saving Face in Relationships

In many Asian societies, respect, honor, and a person's reputation in the community involve giving "face" (*mianzi*). Disrespect results in "losing face" (*diumianzi*). In Chinese culture, "losing face" is an even greater disgrace than shame.

Malachi emphasizes the concept of honoring God – that is, giving "face." A son must honor his father; a slave, his master; and a subject, his king (1:6, 14). By failing to show proper respect in administering the sacrificial system, the priests permit God to lose face in the community. Therefore, God will not accept their offerings (1:6b–10).

The priests who serve in God's temple utter priestly blessings, asking that God's face shine on his people.[1] They plead before God's "face" for favor. But

---

1. See Numbers 6:22–26.

since they do not consider God's "face" (honor), God will not lift his "face" to answer their prayers (1:9). Moreover, their descendants will be cut off. They themselves will be publicly disgraced as if the "dung" from their sacrifices is smeared on the faces as a punishment for dishonoring God (2:3). Since their actions cause God to "lose face," the priests, in turn, will "lose face" in the community.

In Chinese society, showing "face" sometimes results in showing favoritism to one party over another. Malachi 2:9 warns against showing "partiality" (literally, "lifting of face"). The teachers of God's word should not favor one area of his teaching over other areas of his instruction. They must teach the whole counsel of God.

Holistic relationships are important in Asian societies. There must be congruence between who people are ("being") and what they do. In Chinese culture, *guanxi* (relationship) is the key to a blissful life. The popular Chinese saying, "It does not matter if there is a relationship. It does matter if there is no relationship" (*You guanxi jiu meiyou guanxi. Meiyou guanxi jiu you guanxi*), implies that a holistic relationship is vital to sustain one's relationship with others. Messengers of God must guard and maintain the role entrusted to them (2:7). Their hearts, lips, and life should honor God (2:2, 6–8). Being and doing must be integrated in a life that is wholly committed to the Lord. If their walk with God does not match their teaching, they will be despised and humiliated before the people (2:9).

Memory and Remembrance

Memory and remembrance are not about passively depositing facts but are active processes of creating meaning. In Asian cultures, family histories are often passed on in story form to future generations. Confucius's words were handed down through his disciples as "sayings." These sayings continue to be transmitted within the Chinese community. Similarly, within families, the sayings of ancestors and their stories are handed down from generation to generation and may be retold in various ways. Asian church histories are usually oral rather than written history.

The book of Genesis contains many stories that would have been handed down from generation to generation. One example is the story of Jacob and Esau. In this story, Jacob is deceitful and manipulative, while Esau, Isaac's firstborn, is careless and unmindful of the privileges of his birthright. In his first disputation, where the returnees are reminded that God loves them, the prophet Malachi refers to the story of Jacob and Esau (1:2–3). As the postexilic returnees recall God's love for their ancestor Jacob, they are reminded that God loves them, too.

In Asian societies, memory and remembrance may encourage philanthropic acts. For instance, families may donate money to a church or charitable organization so that their loved ones who have passed away may be remembered in the community. In Chinese culture, the benevolent deeds of the dead person may be published in the newspapers or inscribed in some public places. Such written accounts not only ensure remembrance but may also inspire the younger generation to emulate the acts of those who have gone before them. In Malachi, a scroll of remembrance is written concerning those who feared the Lord and honored his name (3:16).

THEOLOGICAL THEMES

Exile is painful for the people of God. The biblical prophets are sometimes classified according to the time period during which they ministered – before, during, or after the Babylonian exile. Preexilic prophets such as Jeremiah, Ezekiel, Nahum, Habakkuk, and Zephaniah prophesied just before or during the exile; exilic prophets like Daniel and Ezekiel prophesied during the time of the exile; and, postexilic prophets like Malachi, Haggai, and Zechariah prophesied after the people's return from the exile. Malachi presents a profound theological message that addresses the distinctive needs of the returnees from the exile. The book has two main theological themes: an unrivaled God and unreliable people.

Unrivaled God

The Lord is majestic and great; he is to be worshiped by all peoples in every nation. God's unrivaled greatness extends beyond Israel's borders and his name will one day be revered among all nations (1:5, 11, 14).

The "Lord Almighty" ("Lord of hosts") appears 24 times in the book of Malachi. This term first appears in the early history of Israel, during the pre-monarchical and monarchical eras (Gen 17:1; Exod 6:3; 1 Sam 1:11). The title, "the Lord Almighty" (or "the Lord of hosts"), portrays God as the ultimate divine warrior who is commander of the heavenly army ("hosts") and the one who fights on behalf of his people. But later in Israel's history, because of the influences of foreign nations, "hosts" was used to refer to the starry hosts; and so, to avoid any possible disrespect to God's sacred name, the title "hosts" fell into disuse.

The God who enters into covenant with his people is also a father to them (1:6; 2:10), their master and great king (1:6, 14), witness to their marriage covenants (2:14), as well as the one who testifies against them and judges their iniquity (3:5; compare Mic 1:2). He is the Lord of history, who controls the rise and fall of nations (1:4–5). He is the Lord who does not change or go back in his covenant (3:6).

Unreliable People

God, in his sovereignty, elected Jacob.[2] As children of Jacob, who had experienced God's grace and mercy, God's people should have followed the Lord wholeheartedly; yet, they have failed to do so (3:7). Despite their privileged status, they doubt God's goodness and dare to question his actions (1:2; 2:17; 3:7–9; 13–14).

UNITY

The unity of the book is apparent in the carefully planned presentation of its message. The entire book is presented in the form of six disputations – that is, a form of one-sided debate between God and people. The first disputation, for example, is about love – whereas the people wonder whether and how God has loved them, God argues that their continued existence and preservation proves his love. Each of the six disputations has a declaration-response-rebuttal structure, which adopts the format, "You say this . . . but I say to you." The purpose of these disputations is to show the people that they should desire God and to teach them the proper response to a loving God. The greatness of God is to be revered, both in Israel and among the nations (1:5, 11, 14).

In addition, the entire book is presented as three prophecies ("oracles" ESV). The three movements in Malachi have the following themes: Respect for the Lord (1:1–2:9); Remain Faithful to the Lord (2:10–3:5); Return to the Lord (3:6–4:3). And the book concludes with a Reminder from the Lord (4:4–6).

The theme of God's covenantal faithfulness that runs through the entire book also demonstrates its unity. God loves Jacob (1:2) and makes a covenant with Levi (2:4–6). He stands as a witness to the marriage covenant between husband and wife (2:10–14). When the people practice evil, God testifies against them to protect the innocent (3:5). He has appointed the priests and Levites as his messengers and entrusts them with delivering his message (2:7). In addition, he will send the messenger of the covenant to prepare the way for

---

2. See commentary on Malachi 1:2.

the day of the Lord (3:1). When the people return to him, he will remember his covenant and shower them with bountiful blessings (3:6–12). God challenges his covenant people to remember and follow the teachings of Moses (4:4), and those who revere God and remain in covenant with him will enjoy his covenant blessing of restoration (4:2). Just as God sent his messenger, he will also send "the prophet Elijah" before the dreadful day of the Lord to warn people to return to the covenant (4:5–6).

USE OF TORAH AND PROPHETIC TRADITION

In expounding his message, Malachi uses several key ideas found in both the Torah and the Prophets. Jacob, the ancestor of Israel, is loved by God (1:2). This links Malachi with Genesis, the first book in the Torah, where Jacob is first mentioned.

The sacrificial system is important in both the Torah and the prophetic tradition. The Torah contains clear instructions about the sacrificial system and specifies what kinds of animals are acceptable offerings. During the ministry of eighth-century prophets like Hosea, some people opposed the idea of sacrifices by eating those sacrifices instead of offering them to God (Hos 8:13). Malachi, too, addresses people who have been negligent about making right offerings and thus fail to honor God (1:6–14).

The theme of the messenger of God (2:7; 3:1) links the book of Malachi with Haggai and Zechariah. God sent Haggai to deliver his message (Hag 1:13). In Zechariah, the messengers who bring night visions are angels (Zech 1:9–14; 4:15; 5:5; 6:4–5). In Malachi, the Lord sends his messenger to prepare the way before him (3:1); in Exodus, the angelic messenger prepares the way for God's people (Exod 23:20–23).

The theme of the "great and dreadful day of the Lord" (4:5) links Malachi with several OT prophets: Joel (2:1), Amos (5:18), Zephaniah (2:2–3), Haggai (2:23), and Zechariah (12:8). Malachi poses the rhetorical question, "Who can endure the day of his coming?" (3:2; see Joel 2:11). God's justice is like a refiner's fire for the righteous (3:3–4) but a dreaded judgment on those who persist in doing evil (3:5).

NEW TESTAMENT CONNECTIONS

Paul cites Malachi 1:2–3: "Jacob I loved, but Esau I hated" (Rom 9:13). It is not because of his own merit that Jacob enjoyed the love of God but because of God's sovereign will. It is the plan of God for the nation of Israel to receive his grace and mercy.

"I will send my messenger, who will prepare the way before me" (3:1). In the New Testament, this messenger is identified as John the Baptist (Mark 1:2). John preaches a message of repentance which is identical to the message of cleansing in Malachi 3:1–5. Jesus also connects John the Baptist with Elijah who comes before the dreadful day of the Lord (4:4–5).[3]

The messenger of the covenant, another messenger, is the Lord who will come to his temple (3:1b). As God's messenger (3:1a) prepares the way, the messenger of the covenant refines and purifies the Levites (3:2–4). In the NT, the messenger of the covenant is identified as Jesus, God's Son, the one sent by the Father (John 3:17; 5:23–24; 8:16).

---

3. See Matthew 11:7–14; Mark 9:11–13; Luke 1:17.

OUTLINE

1:1–2:9 Respect for the Lord

    1:1–5   First Disputation: Doubting God's Love

          1:1   Superscription

          1:2   God's Love Is Tender

          1:3–5   God's Love Is Tough

    1:6–2:9   Second Disputation: Failing to Honor God

          1:6–14   Acceptable Sacrifices

          2:1–9   Acceptable Service

2:10–3:5 Remain Faithful to the Lord

    2:10–16   Third Disputation: Unfaithfulness in Relationships

          2:10   Unfaithfulness Challenged

          2:11–12 Unfaithfulness by Mixed-Faith Marriages

          2:13–16 Unfaithfulness by Divorce

    2:17–3:5 Fourth Disputation: Unrighteousness in Relationships

          2:17   God's Justice Is Questioned

          3:1–4   God's Messenger of Justice

          3:5   Proclamation of God's Justice

3:6–4:3 Return to the Lord

    3:6–12   Fifth Disputation: Grudging Giving to God

          3:6–7   A Gracious God

          3:8–9   The People's Failure to Give Generously

          3:10–12 God's Promise to Bless Abundantly

    3:13–4:3 Sixth Disputation: Arrogant Accusations against God

          3:13–15 The People's Allegations against God

          3:16–4:3 God Answers His People

4:4–6 Conclusion: Reminder from the Lord

MALACHI 1:1–2:9

RESPECT FOR THE LORD

In this first movement, the Lord confronts the people's failure to respect him. They fail to respect God by doubting his love for them (1:1–5) and by their failure to honor him by acceptable sacrifices (1:6–14) and service (2:1–9). The first movement includes two declarations (1:2a, 1:6ab) and two refutations (1:2b, 1:6c–7). Each section includes an emphasis on the greatness of God: his greatness extends beyond the borders of Israel (1:5) and he is worthy of respect among the nations (1:11, 14b).

1:1–5 FIRST DISPUTATION: DOUBTING GOD'S LOVE

The first disputation deals with God's affection for his people. The message is addressed to the people of God who have just returned from exile (1:1). These returnees may have wondered if God still loved them, since he had sent them off to exile. And so Malachi begins with an affirmation of God's love for his people. The reference to Jacob and Esau recalls a familiar story in the book of Genesis. By citing Jacob, the ancestor of Israel, Malachi reminds the people of God's care for Israel throughout history, even in their exile – since he has now brought them safely home (1:2). By contrasting his people's return to their homeland with Esau's land – which God has laid bare and made into a wasteland (1:3–4) – the Lord reminds his people of his love for them. Only his love has preserved them and their land.

God's love is both tender (1:2) and tough (1:3–5). God's covenant people experience his tender love. His tough love is demonstrated against those who refuse to respond to his care and concern.

1:1 Superscription

As in Nahum (Nah 1:1) and Habakkuk (Hab 1:1), the superscription in Malachi simply identifies the genre of the prophetic message and the messenger: "A prophecy: The word of the LORD to Israel through Malachi" (1:1). The word translated "prophecy" or "oracle" (ESV) is *masaʾ*, a term that also appears in a series of prophecies against the nations (Isa 13:1; 15:1; 17:1; 19:1; 21:1; 23:1) and in a collection of sayings in the book of Zechariah (9:1). Oracle means "burden"; the Lord is burdened by his people's accusations against him. The prophet is simply the messenger who delivers God's word to the people.

Malachi, as God's spokesperson, speaks the word of the Lord to Israel. He is the channel of God's message. Israel was the name given to God's people, those who enjoyed a covenantal relationship with the Lord. In the postexilic era, Israel was synonymous with Judah, the remnant who returned from exile (2:11). Those who returned from the exile took the covenantal name, Israel, rather than their tribal identity "Judah." These people are descendants of Jacob, whom God loves (1:2).

1:2 God's Love Is Tender

This first section deals with God's tender affection for his people. The book of Genesis explains the origin of the deep-rooted animosity between Jacob and Esau. These brothers, who were also twins, competed with each other even in the womb. Jacob gained his father's blessing through deceit. Esau, because he had despised his birthright, forfeited the blessing and ended up hating his brother (Gen 27:1–41). Yet, despite Jacob's character flaws, God chose him to receive his blessings (Gen 32:22–32).

The postexilic community, as they return to a ruined land, struggle to comprehend the love of God. Malachi uses the first disputation to emphasize God's love for this returnee community. He begins with the Lord's simple declaration: "I have loved you" (1:2a). The Hebrew grammar implies that the Lord's love – his covenant love which begins early in the history of Israel, as far back as the book of Genesis – is a continuing love, extending even to the postexilic community.

But the returnees doubt God's enduring love for them and ask, "How have you loved us?" (1:2b): Malachi uses a rhetorical question – "Was not Esau Jacob's brother?" (1:2c) – to answer their question. Jacob and Esau represent two nations. Jacob, whose name was changed to "Israel" (Gen 32:28), was the father of the nation Israel. Similarly, Esau was the ancestor of Edom (Gen 36:1). By referring to Jacob by name and affirming his love for Jacob, God was personalizing his love for both the nation of Israel and their forefather.

1:3–5 God's Love Is Tough

While Jacob and the nation of Israel enjoy God's tender love, Esau and Edom experience God's tough love. In 587 BC, Edom joined the pillaging party of Babylonians who raided the Israelites (Ezek 35:1–15; Obad 10–14). Living in the mountains, the Edomites had become arrogant and boastful about the security of their stronghold (Obad 3–4). Because of God's judgment, Edom became a desolate wasteland, inhabited only by desert jackals (1:3).

"I have loved Jacob, but Esau I have hated" (1:2b–3a) is a declaration that troubles many people. If God is a loving God, how can he "hate" some people? Scholars have explained this love-hate pair in three different ways.

First, the love-hate pair is explained in terms of divine sovereign election. God is sovereign, and he may show mercy and compassionate love to whomever he chooses (Exod 33:19). Even before they were born, God demonstrated his sovereignty by choosing Jacob over his twin brother Esau to be the one who inherited the blessing and continued the covenant line of Abraham (Gen 25:23). Because of this election, God brings Jacob's descendants – the Israelites – out of Egypt, makes them his people, and demonstrates his covenant love for them (Deut 4:37; 7:7–8). In the same way, God sovereignly rejects Esau, irrespective of Esau's behavior. These are divine sovereign choices.

Second, the love-hate pair is explained in terms of priority. Jacob's love for Rachel was "greater than his love for Leah" (Gen 29:31). When God sees that "Leah was not loved" (Gen 29:33), he opens up her womb *prior* to Rachel's, showing his love for Leah and protecting the rights of the wife whose husband does not love her.[1] Similarly, God's love for Jacob is explained in terms of priority. Since Isaac, their father, loved Esau more than Jacob, God gave priority to Jacob.

Third, the love-hate pair is explained in terms of covenantal relationship. Since Esau, the firstborn, did not value his birthright (Gen 25:32), God would not enter into a covenantal relationship with him. The firstborn played a significant role in the Israelite community and was entitled to certain rights (1 Chr 5:1–2), including the right to a double share of the father's inheritance that came with the expectation that the firstborn would care for his aging parents (Deut 21:15–17). To forfeit the rights and duties of the firstborn, as Esau did, was a serious offense. Therefore, God did not enter into a covenant with Esau.

Selling his birthright was not Esau's only sin. He also took foreign wives, which displeased the Lord (Gen 26:34–35; 27:46). The NT says that he was "sexually immoral" and "godless" and "for a single meal sold his inheritance rights as the oldest son" (Heb 12:16). Nevertheless, God does not withhold his blessings from Esau. He had already blessed Esau with a gift for hunting and a special bond with his father (Gen 25:27–28). He also makes Esau the founder of a nation – Edom. Esau was the ancestor of the Edomites (Gen

---

1. See Deuteronomy 21:15–17.

36:1). Edom means "red," a possible reference to Esau's hair color (Gen 25:25, 30). God had given Esau and his descendants the hill country of Seir – and Israel was reminded that these people were their "brothers" and warned not to "provoke them to war" (Gen 36:8; Deut 2:4–6). Like Israel, Edom also had twelve tribes and they became a powerful and prosperous nation (Gen 36).

Yet, Edom, like its forefather Esau, displeased God. Edom plotted violence and murder against Israel (Joel 3:19; Obad 10–14), harbored hostility against the Israelites (Ezek 35:5), violated its brotherly obligations towards Israel (Num 20:14–21; Judg 11:17), and was boastful about its military strength and mountain stronghold. Therefore, neither Esau nor the Edomites enjoyed the blessings of God's covenantal love.

In traditional hierarchical Chinese societies, communication tends to flow in one direction only – from top to bottom. Since age and position in the family command respect, younger members of the family are obliged to heed the instructions of their elders. It is common for parents to praise their friends' children but not their own sons and daughters. They may even struggle to express their love for children and grandchildren in meaningful ways. God, however, expresses his love for Israel in deeply meaningful ways, both by his words and by his actions. The Lord wants all people to experience his loving care in positive, upbuilding ways. Let us cultivate a culture in which people can express and experience love in meaningful ways.

LEARNING THE LANGUAGES OF LOVE

The OT concludes with God's promise that when the prophet Elijah comes again, "he will turn the hearts of the parents to their children, and the hearts of the children to their parents," thereby reconciling and restoring strained relationships within families (Mal 4:5–6). The need for such a promise and blessing has never been greater. And this is not only where marriages have broken down or where families are separated because one parent is employed overseas. Because of various cultural factors in Asian societies, relationships between parents and children are sometimes characterized by poor communication and misunderstandings, leading to bitterness and anger. While most Asian parents treasure their children, many struggle to express their love in ways that make children feel loved. We need to find ways to turn the hearts of parents to their children and the hearts of children to their parents.

Gary Chapman, a Christian psychologist, explains that people may express their love in five different ways: giving gifts, spending quality time, words of affirmation, acts of service, and wholesome physical touch.[1] One of the ways Filipinos express love for family is by *beso-beso* – a respectful greeting where children greet their parents and close relatives by kissing their cheeks. As a sign of respect, children also take the hands of the elderly and place them on their own forehead while saying, "mano po" (which means, "respectfully yours"). In traditional Chinese families, love is expressed by service to the family. Parents who provide materially for their family – even if this means working overseas and being separated from the family for long periods – are regarded by society as loving parents. It is important to understand how different cultures express love for family members. But it is also vital to ask ourselves whether such expressions of love are interpreted as love by our children.

In honor-shame cultures, there is a tendency to "shame" children into behaving in particular ways. This is not emotionally healthy and can lead to children feeling that they must "earn" or "deserve" their parents' love. Instead, parents must learn the languages of love by which they can express unconditional love for their children in meaningful ways: by words of love and praise for who their children are as well as for their achievements; by hugs, kisses, and loving touch; by thoughtful gifts; by sacrificial acts of service; and by spending quality time with their children.

At the beginning of Malachi, God declares his love for the postexilic community (1:2a); he assures them of his fatherly compassion and calls them his "treasured possession" (3:17); and the book closes with God's exhortation to his people to "remember the law" (4:4). As children feel loved and affirmed, they are more likely to obey their parents.

1. Gary Chapman, *The 5 Love Languages: The Secret to Love that Lasts*, reprint (Chicago: Northfield Publishing, 2015).

1:6–2:9 SECOND DISPUTATION: FAILING TO HONOR GOD

In his second disputation, Malachi deals with the failures of priests and people to honor God. The sacrificial system was given to the people as a way to respond to God's love. It also provided a way to restore their relationship with God. The Torah clearly set out the responsibilities of the priests and Levites. This second disputation is addressed to the priests (1:6; 2:1) and is a direct message from "the LORD Almighty" (1:6, 8, 10, 11, 12, 14; 2:2, 8). The priests mediated the sacrificial offerings at the altar and were also entrusted with teaching God's message (2:7).

The preexilic or eighth-century prophets – Isaiah, Hosea, Amos, and Micah – emphasized the social and ethical responsibilities of the community. For these prophets, loving God meant showing love to the community, especially the poor and needy.[2] They focused on radical obedience to the word of God and did not place great emphasis on the worship life of the people. Any mention of worship regulations was usually in relation to criticisms of the sacrificial system and the priests. Malachi, however, as a postexilic prophet, is greatly concerned about the purity of worship and its rituals. The rebuilding of the temple during the postexilic era gave the people the opportunity to worship God in Jerusalem. Worship was a way to show love and respect for God in response to his bountiful blessings, and the priests were charged with administering the sacrificial system and teaching the people the right way to worship God.

2. There are five models of prophetic spirituality: the "Commitment Model," "Ascetic Model," "Mystical Model," "Contemplative Model," and "Community Model." The latter deals with spirituality demonstrated through love for people in need. See Joseph Too Shao, "Spirituality in the Prophetic Traditions: An Asian Perspective," in *Perjuangan Menatung Zaman (Kumpulan esai sebagai penghargaan kepada Pendeta Stephen Tong, pada HUT ke-60, Festschrift for Stephen Tong)*, ed. Hendra G. Mulia (Jakarta: Reformed Institute Press, 2000), 125–150.

The disputation comprises a dialogue between God and the priests. God accuses the priests of dishonoring him in two ways. First, instead of acceptable offerings, they offer defiled animals on the altar. The Lord would rather close the temple doors than accept these sacrifices (1:6–14). Second, they dishonor him by failure to render acceptable service of teaching God's word faithfully. Instead of preserving and passing on knowledge and instruction to God's people, the teaching of the priests has caused the people to stumble (2:1–9).

1:6–14 Acceptable Sacrifices

During the postexilic period, in the time of the prophets Haggai and Zechariah, the temple of God was rebuilt by the first group of returnees (Ezra 6:13–22). With the temple established as the place of worship, the postexilic community were expected to show due respect for God, and one way to do this was through acceptable sacrifices that demonstrated their love and respect. The priests were charged with ensuring that the people brought the right gifts and offerings.

The second disputation uses a declaration-response-rebuttal cycle to bring a charge against the priests. In dealing with the issue of honor, two relationships are examined. The first involves a son and his father: "A son honors his father" (1:6). Honoring one's parents was both a key value within Israelite society and one of the Ten Commandments – a commandment that promised the blessing of long life (Exod 20:12; Deut 5:16; see also Eph 6:2–3). To honor one's parents involved listening to their instructions (Prov 1:8; 13:1), and disobedient children were punished publicly at the city gate (Deut 21:18–21). The second relationship involves a slave and his master (1:6). Slaves were required to honor and respect their masters. Since God is both their father and their king (Deut 32:6; Exod 34:23), the people of God must honor him. The priests, as leaders in the community, are expected to model for the people how to honor and respect God.

In the OT, worship begins with Abel's offering (Gen 4:3–4). Later, Noah builds an altar and sacrifices clean animals and birds in gratitude to God for his protection (Gen 8:20). In response to God's love, Abraham builds altars where he worships God (Gen 12:7–8; 13:18). Similarly, Moses builds an altar to thank God for defeating the Amalekites (Exod 17:15). At Mount Sinai, God institutes the three annual festivals which will be part of Israel's liturgical calendar (Exod 23:14–19).

After the construction of the tabernacle, the Lord instructs Moses on how the sacrificial system is to be set up (Lev 1–7) and chooses Jerusalem as the city where these annual feasts are to be celebrated (Deut 12:14). Temple worship begins after Solomon builds the first temple (1 Kgs 9:25), which he dedicates to the Lord (2 Chr 7:5). The pattern of daily, weekly, monthly, and annual ceremonies with sacrifices are followed in temple worship. Additional duties are assigned to the priests and Levites (2 Chr 8:13–14) and, in the postexilic community, the priests play a key role in matters relating to God's law (Hag 2:11–12). They are expected to know the Torah and faithfully instruct the returnees about the various rituals and regulations of worship.

God's name must be honored (Exod 20:7). By failing to offer proper gifts to God, the priests demonstrate contempt for God's name and defile God's altar. They did not learn their lesson from what happened to Aaron's sons when they failed to honor God at the altar (Lev 10:1–3). Malachi confronts the priests, pointing out that blemished offerings dishonor the Lord who is their "great king" and whose "name is to be feared among the nations" (1:14b).

Asian societies are pluralistic in their religious beliefs. For instance, in Bali, Indonesia, early each morning the women prepare food for their household gods. In Kathmandu, Nepal, where many gods are worshiped, people visit the temple of their choice to plead for favors from the gods. In Chinese societies, worshipers offer gifts at Buddhist or Taoist temples on auspicious days in the lunar calendar.

In contract to the varying customs and styles of worship in Asian religions, God gives clear guidelines for how he is to be worshiped. Detailed instructions about the OT sacrificial system – that is, what constituted acceptable sacrifices and how these offerings were to be made – were given to both people and priests (Lev 1–7). God's people, regardless of their social standing or wealth, were required to bring various kinds of offerings to the Lord. Their offerings of sacrificial animals were referred to as "food" (Lev 21:6, 8, 21) and worshipers had to ensure that these animals were "without defect" (Lev 1:3, 10). The priests were charged with safeguarding the holiness of the sacrificial system and teaching the people how to worship their holy God. Since offering blemished animals dishonored God, Aaron and his sons were commanded not to accept animals that were defective in any way (Lev 22:17–25). The worshipers were to bring the prescribed sacrifices and the priests were to ensure that these were acceptable before they offered these gifts at the altar.

During the postexilic era, the priests knew what had been prescribed in the Torah about acceptable offerings. By failing to comply with these requirements, they show contempt for God. Malachi challenges the priests to consider how they would honor the governor, their political leader. They would not dream of offering substandard offerings to the governor and he would not be pleased with them if they did! Neither will God accept mediocre gifts from his people.

The role of the priests was not only to offer acceptable sacrifices but also to intercede with God on behalf of the worshipers and to mediate God's blessing to the people (Num 6:22–27). In the OT, worshipers would bring their offerings to God along with their prayer requests (Ps 20:1–5). As the all-powerful Creator of the universe, God owns everything and needs nothing, yet he establishes the sacrificial system as a way for people to respond to his love (Ps 50:7–15). Therefore, God's people must worship him with the right attitude (Isa 1:10–17; Amos 5:21–24). When the priests approached the altar with blemished offerings or wrong attitudes, they failed to honor God, and so their pleas that God be gracious to his people will go unheard. Their prayers and offerings on behalf of the people will not be accepted by God (1:9). The priests' failure to carry out their duties is so serious that the Lord will no longer accept their service in the temple. He declares that it would be better to "shut the temple doors" rather than to continue to "light useless fires" and offer worthless sacrifices (1:10; see Isa 1:13).

In the closing verses of this section on honoring God through acceptable sacrifices, the greatness of God is twice emphasized (1:11, 14). God is not only a father and master who must be honored (1:6), he is also "a great king" whose name is to be "feared among the nations" (1:14). Revering God means worshiping him in a fitting manner and with a right spirit. One day, God's greatness will be acknowledged by all nations and he will be honored and worshiped everywhere – "from where the sun rises to where it sets" (Pss 50:1; 113:3) – with acceptable offerings (1:11). In contrast, the priests in Malachi's time show contempt for God by permitting careless worship that does not please the Lord (1:12–14; see also 1:6–7). To offer "injured, lame or diseased animals" (1:13) – which were not even fit for human consumption and were usually thrown to the dogs (Exod 22:31) – was to insult God. To offer a blemished animal when fulfilling a vow was to "cheat" God and bring down a curse on oneself (1:14a).

To honor God is to recognize and revere his greatness which extends "beyond the borders of Israel" (1:5). And one day, people everywhere, in every nation, will acknowledge the greatness of God and adore him as the King of kings (1:11, 14; see also Phil 2:9–11).

GIVING THAT HONORS GOD

The postexilic community of Malachi's time were oblivious to the gravity of their sin of withholding "tithes and offerings" from God. When the Lord accuses them of robbing him, they ask, "How are we robbing you?" (3:8). The people were robbing God of the honor due to him by failing to give graciously, gratefully, and generously.

While the NT has no specific rules and regulations about tithes and offerings, it does teach that generous giving is a vital aspect of our worship of God. For example, Paul tells the Corinthians: "Remember this: Whoever sows sparingly will also reap sparingly, and whoever sows generously will also reap generously. Each of you should give what you have decided in your heart to give, not reluctantly or under compulsion, for God loves a cheerful giver. And God is able to bless you abundantly, so that in all things at all times, having all that you need, you will abound in every good work" (2 Cor 9:6–8).

This attitude of generosity is not alien to Asian cultures. Most Asians consider hospitality an important virtue and love to bless family and friends with their gifts. So it is not difficult to teach and encourage believers to let this same generosity spill over into their giving to God's work. But sometimes, Asians give because they feel obliged to do so or out of a spirit of rivalry that seeks to give a "better" gift than someone else. Our giving to God should not be marked by such attitudes. We are not called to give grudgingly – simply out of a sense of duty – but because we delight to give back to God a small portion of what he has graciously given us.

Even when poverty prevents people from giving gifts of money, they can still give of their time or talents – these, too, are important offerings. At the same time, giving that honors God is not simply giving out of our excess. As King David said, "I will not sacrifice to the LORD my God burnt offerings that cost me nothing" (2 Sam 24:24). God is not interested in the monetary value of our offerings, but he does care whether we give sacrificially. That is why Jesus placed such great value on a poor widow's offering of two copper coins (Mark 12:41–44).

2:1–9 Acceptable Service

In the postexilic era, the priests played a vital role. They had a dual responsibility. Not only were they to offer sacrifices, they were also to teach the people (2:7). So it was important that the priests were obedient to God and honored his name by faithfully fulfilling their role in both the sacrificial system and the teaching ministry. But in Malachi's time, the priests have failed to offer acceptable service to God. This section begins with a harsh warning (2:1–4), followed by a reminder of God's covenant with the priestly tribe of Levi (2:5–7), and concludes with a stern rebuke of the priests (2:8–9).

Malachi begins by warning the priests that if they will not listen and fulfill their God-given responsibilities, they will be severely punished (2:1–2). To set one's heart or to be "resolved" (2:2) implies determination and commitment. In OT psychology, the heart was the decision-making organ (Deut 6:4; Prov 4:23). If the priests do not set their hearts on honoring God, they cannot be channels of his grace in their teaching ministry. The consequences will be severe: "I will send a curse on you, and I will curse your blessings" (2:2). In Deuteronomy, a curse was intended to bring people back to God so that they might experience his blessings once more. In the exile, the returnees had experienced the wrath of God as various covenant curses were invoked (Deut 28:15–68). The priests are now warned that their disobedience would also invite divine curses. The act of blessing was part of the priestly vocation (Deut 21:5; Num 6:22–27); but now, even their blessings would be cursed – their daily priestly blessing would become anti-blessing.[3]

Since the priests have failed to honor God, now *they* will be dishonored. God will punish the priests in two ways. First, the "rebuke" of their descendants suggests that their priestly line will not continue (2:3a). Second, God will terminate their services and they will be disgraced before the people (2:3b). When animals were offered as festival sacrifices, their entrails and internal organs (commonly called "offal") were thrown and burned outside the camp (2:3; Exod 29:14; Lev 8:17). Offal is smelly and dirty. To have offal ("dung" NIV) spread on their faces is not only embarrassing for the priests but renders them unclean and hence unfit to serve. The fate of the priests would be the same as that of the unclean offal which is carried outside the camp and burned. When Eli failed to honor God, his sons died and his family were cut off from serving God (1 Sam 2:29–34); similarly, the priests who dishonored God

---

3. Jonathan Gibson, "Covenant Continuity and Fidelity in Malachi," *TynBul* 66 (2015): 314–315.

would no longer be able to serve as priests and would have no descendants to carry on the family name.

God reminds the priests of the "covenant of life and peace" he had made with Levi (2:5a). This covenant of perpetual priesthood had been made with the Levitical priest Phinehas – a grandson of Aaron – because of his zeal for God (Num 25:11–13; Neh 13:29). Life and peace are both blessings from God, and the expression suggests not merely long life but the fullness of life that is promised in this covenant. The priests, in turn, must respond by revering God and honoring his name (2:5).

The priests are called to be faithful by knowing God's law, living the law by a lifestyle of integrity, and diligently teaching the law (2:6–7; compare Ezra 7:10). By walking with God "in peace and uprightness," the priests testify to the trustworthiness of God's teaching and accomplish the goal of true instruction, which is to turn many from sin (2:6b; compare Dan 12:3; Jas 5:20). The priests must also "preserve knowledge" (2:7a). In the OT, knowledge is not just knowing facts or information but refers to an experiential understanding of God that leads to the application of God's truth to one's life. The priests must experience and live out God's truth and then instruct the people in this truth, so that they, too, can experience God in their own lives (2:7). As God's messengers, the priests' words carry authority, since it is God's word that they teach the people.

Malachi returns once more to the situation during the postexilic period. The priests have not lived up to their high and holy calling (2:8–9; see 2:2). Instead of faithfully instructing the people in the truth and turning many from sin (2:6–7), the priests themselves have turned away from God and stumbled into sin; and because of their poor example and shortcomings in their teaching – including "partiality in matters of the law" – they have caused the people to stumble (2:8). Because the priests have violated the covenant with Levi, failed to follow God's ways, and showed partiality in matters of the law, God subjects them to public humiliation and disgrace (2:9).

The late Rev. Wesley K. Shao – who served as the senior pastor of the United Evangelical Church of the Philippines for more than three decades – took the pulpit ministry extremely seriously. When selecting biblical passages or themes on which to preach on each week, he prayerfully sought God's direction and was able to discern the needs of God's people because of his weekly home visitations. When sharing the pulpit ministry with other pastors, he carefully and prayerfully assessed their background and ensured that they were grounded in sound doctrine.

If the priests of Malachi's time had offered acceptable service, the postexilic worshipers would have honored the Lord with acceptable sacrifices. Pastors and teachers – who are the modern-day priests and scribes – should not only know the word and teach the word but also apply it wholeheartedly in all areas of their lives. It is then that their ministries will help people to know the truth and follow the Lord.

MALACHI 2:10–3:5

REMAIN FAITHFUL TO THE LORD

The second movement addresses two issues. First, God confronts his people's unfaithful relationships (2:10–16). Faithfulness in marriage is vital and faithful marital unions result in a generation of godly offspring (2:15). Second, God addresses unrighteousness or injustice (2:17–3:5). God's people must remain faithful even in difficult times. The God of justice will purify those who serve him (3:3–4) and punish the wicked (3:5). The purpose of both disputations is to urge the people of God to be faithful.

2:10–16 THIRD DISPUTATION: UNFAITHFULNESS IN RELATIONSHIPS

God cares about families. He wants husbands and wives to be faithful in marriage. This was God's design for marriage from the very beginning (Gen 2:18–25). As those who worship the one Creator, as those who are children of one Father, God's people must demonstrate their faithfulness to him by remaining faithful to one another. When God's people marry women who worship foreign gods, they are being unfaithful to the God of the covenant (2:11–12). When they divorce their wives, their covenant partners in marriage, their unfaithfulness displeases God (2:13–16).

2:10 Unfaithfulness Challenged

Malachi begins this section with two rhetorical questions: "Do we not all have one Father? Did not one God create us?" (2:10a). Both questions must be answered in the affirmative: Yes, God is both the Father who cares for Israel, his firstborn (Exod 4:22–23), and the Creator who formed them. Malachi then rebukes the people: "Why do we profane the covenant of our ancestors by being unfaithful to one another?" (2:10b). Since God's people are in a kinship relationship with God and with one another, these kinship ties must be cherished and protected. Malachi addresses two specific issues: mixed-faith marriages (2:11–12) and divorce (2:13–16).

2:11–12 Unfaithfulness by Mixed-Faith Marriages

A serious accusation is brought against the people: "Judah has been unfaithful" (2:11a). But how should we interpret the marriage imagery in these verses? Some scholars see this as referring to unholy alliances between Israel and the surrounding nations. Others interpret it typologically, as idolatry – which is spiritual adultery. A third approach takes this literally, seeing "the detestable thing" as intermarriage with those who worshiped other gods.[1] The first two views do not have much support and most scholars favor the third interpretation.

Marriage is depicted as sacred (*qodesh*; "sanctuary" in NIV). The root meaning of *qodesh* is holiness or being set apart for a deity. The union between husband and wife is holy to the Lord, something set apart for the Lord. That is why God requires that his people only marry those of the same faith – that is, those who worship the Lord.

The application of Torah, the law of God, is always countercultural and practical. Even during the time of Moses, God permitted daughters to receive an inheritance (Num 27:1–11). But, in order to safeguard that inheritance, they were required to marry within their own tribe (Num 36:1–13). In the postexilic community, a new problem arose as returnees intermarried and failed to keep themselves "separate from the neighboring peoples with their detestable practices" (Ezra 9:1–2). This was clearly forbidden in the Torah (Deut 7:1–4) because it would endanger the purity of their faith (Exod 34:16).[2] Malachi applies the Lord's instruction to this new situation that has arisen in the postexilic period.

Marrying spouses who worshiped other gods was regarded as a defiling practice because it would lead to syncretism, mixing worship of Yahweh with the worship of other gods (Ezra 10:18–44; Neh 13:23–27).[3] What is prohibited here is not marriage between people of different races. In the megacities of Asia, we see more and more mixed marriages.[4] As Asians migrate and work in other countries, they intermarry with people of other races and diaspora communities are forming in almost every part of the world. But what God

---

1. Andrew E. Hill, *Malachi. A New Translation with Introduction and Commentary*, AYBC (New York: Doubleday, 1998), 228.
2. For more discussion on the related issues, see Joseph Too Shao and Rosa Ching Shao, *Ezra and Nehemiah*, ABCS (Carlisle, Cumbria: Langham Global Library, 2019), 86–87.
3. Joseph Too Shao and Rosa Ching Shao, *Ezra and Nehemiah*, 97–100, 206–207.
4. For issues related to intermingling within the diaspora community, see Sadiri Joy Tira and Juliet Uytanlet, *A Hybrid World: Diaspora, Hybridity, and Missio Dei* (Littleton, CO: William Carey, 2020).

hates is unions between God's people and those who worship other gods. Israel's history illustrates the problems of inter-religious marriages. It is important that the returnees remain faithful to God's covenant by making wise choices about marriage.

The guiding principle here in Malachi is very clear: Christian marriage is between two people who worship the same God. Paul echoes the same teaching when he writes, "Do not be yoked together with unbelievers" (2 Cor 6:14a).

The Lord will "remove" offenders from the "tents of Jacob" even though they may bring offerings (2:12). To "remove" is to "cut off" from relationship (1 Kgs 14:10). This is a reminder that violating God's laws has grave consequences (Lev 7:20–21; 17:4, 9). The term "tents of Jacob" refers to the community of Israel who worship the Lord. In the second disputation, the people's offerings of polluted animals were unacceptable (1:7–8). Their polluted lifestyle of intermarriage is also unacceptable and will result in their being cut off from the community of God's people.

2:13–16 Unfaithfulness by Divorce

In this section Malachi deals with another act of unfaithfulness: divorce. This is a matter of great concern to God, who ordained the creation of the family even before he designed the community.

Judah's predicament is stated first: "You flood the LORD's altar with tears. You weep and wail because he no longer looks with favor on your offerings or accepts them with pleasure from your hands" (2:13). The people are upset that the Lord does not accept their offerings or look with favor on them. If God takes no pleasure in their offerings, their sacrifices cannot restore relationship with God (compare 1:10, 13).

Malachi states that the reason their offerings are not accepted is because of their unfaithfulness to their marriage covenants to which the Lord himself has been a witness (2:14). A witness is not a mere spectator during the marriage ceremony but a key participant who testifies to the legality and validity of that marriage.

Malachi gives three descriptions of the wife, each preceded by the possessive pronoun "your" (2:14). First, she is the wife of "your youth," implying that the man married her early in life. A happy married life between husband and wife is likened to running water, overflowing springs, and a fountain that satisfies, blesses, and brings mutual enjoyment to both husband and wife (Prov 5:15–18). Their marital relationship is intended to be refreshing and life-giving. Second, she is "your partner" (literally, "companion"), which means that the couple is joined together for the purpose of enjoying companionship and helping each other face the challenges of life (Eccl 4:9–12). Third, she is the wife of "your marriage covenant." Husband and wife are bound together in a covenant that is established by divine sanction (Prov 2:17; Ezek 16:8). The wife is not inferior to the husband but is his covenant partner.

Continuing his argument, the prophet asks a rhetorical question: "Has not the one God made you?" (2:15a). As before (2:10), the question demands an affirmative answer: "You belong to him in body and spirit" (2:15b). This refers to the union of husband and wife in the paradigmatic marriage of Genesis 2:22–24. It is the best argument against polygamous relationships. The people of God have one Father and one Creator who made them one (2:10). As God blesses human beings and calls them to be fruitful and multiply, he creates only one helper for the man (Gen 1:28; 2:18). The desire for another woman is against God's creation design. Recognizing God's role as a "witness" (2:14), the people of God must honor their marriage covenants and the bond between husband and wife must not be dissolved.[5]

The one God, who established this covenant of marriage, desires that married couples produce godly offspring (2:15b). Children are gifts from the Lord (Ps 127:3), and parents are entrusted with the sacred duty of raising faithful descendants who love the Lord. In this way, the family of believers will grow. We see this attitude in Abraham, who sent his servant to find a godly wife for his son Isaac (Gen 24:1–4). Malachi appeals to husbands to be watchful, so that they might remain faithful to their wives. Thus marital faithfulness is emphasized.

The next verse on divorce (2:16) has been understood in different ways. Most of the older versions of the Bible translate this, "I hate divorce," with God as the speaker, implying that God hates divorce (KJV, NIV 1984, NASB, NRSV). The Hebrew Bible, however, does not support this translation as the Hebrew text says, "He hates divorce." Some have understood this "he" as a reference to God, which would mean that God hates divorce. Others have understood this "he" as referring to the husband, as in NIV: "The man who hates and divorces his wife." The Greek version of the OT adopts a similar understanding: "But if you, while hating, divorce your wife." Some have even translated this "divorce is hateful,"[6] focusing on the horror of divorce itself.

---

5. Markus Zehnder, "A Fresh Look at Malachi II 13–16," *VT* 53 (2003): 247.

6. David L. Petersen, *Zechariah 9–14 and Malachi*, OTL (Louisville: Westminster, 1995), 205.

Since Malachi emphasizes the importance of companionship (2:14) and godly offspring (2:15), verse 16 could be viewed as a prescriptive statement: God hates that the postexilic people were divorcing the wives of their youth to marry women of other faiths. By alluding to the one flesh union of Genesis 2:24, Malachi urges the people to be faithful in marriage.

The man who divorces his wife is said to do "violence to the one he should protect" (2:16b). The NIV footnote says, "the man who divorces his wife covers his garment with violence." In the OT, to spread one's garment over another symbolized marriage (Ruth 3:9; Ezek 16:8). Divorce was viewed as doing great harm to the marriage covenant. Although the Mosaic law has sometimes been interpreted as permitting divorce, the purpose of these provisions was to prevent a husband from rushing into a decision about divorce and to protect a wife who had been thus divorced (Deut 24:1–4; see also Jer 3:1). Such provisions must be interpreted on the basis of God's original design of marriage as a permanent, lifelong union between one man and one woman. Physical and verbal abuse are not the only kinds of violence that take place within a marriage – abandonment of a spouse is also a form of abuse, while divorce causes great harm and hurt to a spouse.

The final exhortation, "be on your guard, and do not be unfaithful" (2:16b), echoes Malachi's initial cry against unfaithfulness within the community of God's people (2:10). This warning is not just for the people of Malachi's day; it applies equally to modern readers.

WHAT GOD SAYS ABOUT
MARRIAGE AND DIVORCE

"Marriage should be honored by all, and the marriage bed kept pure, for God will judge the adulterer and all the sexually immoral" (Heb 13:4). The whole world has just one Creator, one Father, and one true God (2:10; Rom 3:29). Malachi portrays marriage as a sacred "sanctuary" (2:11) and condemns the treachery of postexilic Jewish men who abandoned their marriage covenant to marry women of other religions. Christians must honor God by upholding the sanctity of marriage.

The NT gives only two possible grounds for divorce: sexual immorality (Matt 5:32; 19:9)[1] and desertion by an unbelieving spouse (1 Cor 7:12–15). Sexual immorality is generally understood to refer to adultery or extramarital affairs.[2] Jesus reiterates the importance of the one flesh union (Matt 19:4–6); hence sexual sin against a spouse includes homosexuality, bestiality, and incest. Jesus also makes it clear that divorce is never a command, only a permission reluctantly given because of the hardness of human hearts (Matt 19:7–8).

The second grounds for divorce is desertion by an unbelieving spouse (1 Cor 7:12–16). Paul makes it clear that when the unbelieving spouse does not wish to leave the marriage, the believing spouse must not seek divorce (7:12–14). Staying together leaves open the possibility that the unbeliever and any children of the marriage may come to Christ. But if the unbelieving spouse chooses to leave, the believer may let the spouse go (7:15–16). This, too, is not a command but only a permission or concession.

In addition to these specific biblical grounds, there may be other valid reasons – such as abandonment or physical, sexual, or emotional abuse and violence – which sometimes make divorce unavoidable.[3] Abandonment – whether husbands abandon their wives or wives their husbands – is also a form of abuse.[4] In some Asian societies, traveling businessmen have wives or mistresses in their various places of business; and this also amounts to abandonment of the spouse to whom they are legally married.

The Asian divorce rate is fast catching up with the global divorce rate. But for God's people, divorce is never a decision to be taken lightly and the sanctity of marriage can never be overemphasized. Churches must be committed to good marriage preparation programs, grounded in solid biblical teaching, while also providing ongoing support for married couples. At the first hint of trouble, husbands and wives should be encouraged to seek counseling. The marriage covenant is to be held in honor by all Christians (Heb 13:4) and the marriage bond should never be entered into casually or dissolved lightly.

---

1. Note the difference between Matthew 19:1–12 and Mark 10:1–12. Whereas Mark 10:11 says, "Anyone who divorces his wife and marries another woman commits adultery against her." Matthew 19:9 says, "Anyone who divorces his wife, *except for sexual immorality*, and marries another woman commits adultery" (italics added). This exception cautions against someone quickly divorcing his wife but permits divorce for sexual immorality. Moses permitted divorce because of one's hardness of heart (Matt 19:8); even in immorality, one may exercise softness of heart and not resort to divorce.
2. Samson Uytanlet with Kiem-Kiok Kwa, *Matthew: A Pastoral and Contextual Commentary*, ABCS (Carlisle, Cumbria: Langham Global Library, 2017), 200.
3. Rebecca Florence Miller, "When Does the Bible Allow Divorce?" *Christianity Today*, April, 2016. See https://www.christianitytoday.com/ct/2016/april-web-only/when-does-bible-allow-divorce.html, accessed October 13, 2020.
4. Solomon O. Ademiluka, "'For I Hate Divorce,' says the Lord: Interpreting Malachi 2:16 in relation to Prohibition of Divorce in Some Churches in Nigeria," OTE 32 (2019): 846–868.

2:17–3:5 FOURTH DISPUTATION:
UNRIGHTEOUSNESS IN RELATIONSHIPS

The fourth disputation focuses on the people's unrighteousness and their presumptuousness in accusing God of condoning evil. The people question God's justice (2:17). God responds by promising to send a messenger who will prepare the way for the coming of the Lord by purifying his covenant people (3:1–4). But the Lord's coming will also be a day of trial and judgment for those who persist in unrighteousness (3:5).

2:17 God's Justice Is Questioned

The people have questioned God's love (1:2–5), failed to honor him (1:6–2:9), and been unfaithful in their relationships (2:10–16). Now they question God's justice (2:17; see also 3:13–15). Yet, they do not even seem aware of the gravity of their own wrongdoing. God's weariness suggests that he is running out of patience.

The accusation, "All who do evil are good in the eyes of the LORD, and he is pleased with them" (2:17b), implies that God is failing to act justly because he allows the wicked to prosper. "Where is the God of justice?" is that age old question of why bad things happen to good people and why good things happen to bad people. But while the people complain about the lack of justice in a world where evil prospers, they fail to see themselves as part of the problem of evil that God must deal with.

3:1–4 God's Messenger of Justice

The Lord's response to the people's accusations is both a promise and a warning. The promise is that of a messenger who will prepare the way for the coming of the Lord of justice, the one whom they seek (3:1). But it is also a warning about the "day of his coming," a day which no human being can endure (3:2–3b). In Malachi 3:1, there are three distinct figures: the messenger who will prepare the way, the Lord himself, and the messenger of the covenant.[7]

---

7. Scholars have suggested either a two-character or a three-character approach. The two-character approach identifies a messenger and the Lord who is also "the messenger of the covenant." But this commentary adopts the three-character approach, treating the figures as distinct: a messenger, the Lord himself, and the messenger of the covenant. This approach has a Christological emphasis since it equates the Messiah ("the messenger of the covenant") with the Lord himself. Andrew S. Malone, "Is the Messiah Announced in Malachi 3:1?," *TynBul* 57 (2006): 227–228. For a scholarly discussion of the related debate and interpretation, see Hill, *Malachi*, 286–289.

God will send a messenger to prepare his way. This could be for the simple purpose of ensuring a safe journey. In the book of Exodus, God's messenger signifies his presence, protection, and power as he leads the people of God to the promised land (Exod 23:20–30). Similarly, God's messenger prepares the way for God's people to return to Jerusalem to serve him (Isa 40:1–5; 57:14). Both the first exodus from Egypt and the second exodus from exile depict God's deliverance. Malachi, however, uses the messenger imagery in the context of judgment. The messenger prepares the people of God for the coming of the God of justice.

The NT points to John the Baptist as the messenger who prepares the way for the Lord Jesus (Matt 3:1–3). John, the Lord's forerunner, is also identified with the prophet Elijah who comes before that "great and dreadful day of the LORD" (4:5; Matt 11:14; 17:10–13). As God's messenger, John the Baptist clears away the obstacles to unbelief.

The one who suddenly appears in his temple is "the Lord"; also identified as "the messenger of the covenant" (3:1). He is distinct from "the LORD Almighty" who speaks and sends his messenger (3:1) and who will come to judge (3:5). The phrase "the messenger of the covenant" is unique, appearing just once in the Bible. Early Jewish writings identified this figure as a heavenly or spiritual being rather than a human being. The writings of the early church fathers identified "the messenger of the covenant" as Jesus Christ. The NT reveals that the messenger of the covenant is Jesus, God's Son, the one "sent" by God (John 3:17; 5:23–24; 8:16) and "the day of his coming" refers to the day of the Lord – which is the day of judgment.

This "messenger" is connected with the covenant (3:1). Since Malachi speaks of a covenant with Levi (2:4, 8), some scholars interpret "covenant" here as the covenant community of Israel and see the messenger as dispensing both covenant blessings and vengeance.[8] This interpretation, however, is highly debatable.

It is more likely that the writer is referring to the "new covenant" (Jer 31:31–34; Ezek 36:26–28). The immediate context of theodicy (the problem of divine and human justice) seems to allude to this new covenant.[9] The first "messenger" serves as the forerunner of the Lord's own return to his temple to establish the new covenant. The NT writers see these two figures – the coming Lord and the messenger of the covenant – as representing the Messiah.

---

8. Peter A. Verhoef, *Haggai and Malachi*, NICOT (Grand Rapids: Eerdmans, 1987), 289.
9. Hill, *Malachi*, 285.

The messenger of the covenant comes to "refine" and to "purify" (3:2–4). Malachi uses two metaphors: the refiner's fire and the launderer's soap (3:2). The intense heat of the refiner's fire refines gold and silver by separating base elements from these precious metals. After purification, these precious metals are used to create beautiful and useful objects. The purging of impurities makes the gold and silver more valuable. Similarly, God's people must endure the painful process of discipline that purifies and brings out the best in them. The second metaphor, the launderer's soap, suggests a strong cleanser such as borax, an alkaline cleansing agent that washes and bleaches clothes until they are spotless.

The Lord longs for justice and righteousness in society. In the postexilic period, both the people of God and the priests had dishonored God by offering unacceptable sacrifices (1:6–14) and rendering unacceptable service (2:1–9). The refining process begins with the Levites – the spiritual leaders of the community – so that the sacrificial system will be purified and the people of God will once again bring offerings that are pleasing in God's sight (3:3–4).

3:5 Proclamation of God's Justice

The people had asked, "Where is the God of justice?" (2:17). Like a judge in a courtroom, the Lord now affirms, "I will come to put you on trial" (3:5a). Like a witness in a lawsuit, he will "be quick to testify" (3:5b) against them. Certain standards of behavior are expected of God's covenant people. Failure to live according to these standards will be judged.

Malachi speaks of two groups of people who will experience God's judgment. The first group – sorcerers, adulterers, and perjurers – are guilty of unfaithfulness in their relationships with God, their spouse, or their community. The second group are guilty of social injustice because they oppress the powerless – the widows and the fatherless – in society.

Sorcerers are those who practice magic. They are condemned both by the Mosaic law (Exod 22:18; Lev 20:27; Deut 18:14) and by the prophets (Jer 27:9; Ezek 13:17–21). This practice leads people astray by occult means, drawing them away from worshiping the true God. Adulterers are to be put to death (Lev 20:10; Deut 22:22) since adultery is an assault against the God-ordained sanctity of marriage (Gen 2:18–24). The Ten Commandments condemn perjurers (Exod 20:16; Deut 5:20) and so do the prophets (Jer 7:9; Zech 5:3–4). Swearing falsely undermines trust in society; by such actions, God's name is taken in vain.

Justice and love for the poor are repeatedly emphasized in the OT. The law denounces those who oppress widows and the fatherless (Exod 22:22–24; Deut 24:19–22) and foreigners (Exod 22:21). Such actions do not demonstrate fear of God. Those who fear God must worship him with clean hands and a pure heart (Pss 15:2–5; 24:4).

C. S. Lewis wrote, "Pain insists upon being attended to. God whispers to us in our pleasures, speaks in our consciences, but shouts in our pains. It is his megaphone to rouse a deaf world."[10] God sometimes uses the trials of life to direct us to act justly, to love mercy, and to walk humbly before him (Mic 6:8). Nevertheless, we should always remember the Lord's promise that he will return. This return will not only bring grace and mercy but also God's justice and righteousness. Are we prepared for this coming?

---

10. C. S Lewis, *The Problem of Pain* (OCR, 1940; New York: Macmillan Company, 1947; repr., Quebec: Samizdat University Press, 2016), 57–58.

MALACHI 3:6–4:3

RETURN TO THE LORD

The third movement consists of two disputations against the people of God. The first of these, which is the fifth disputation in the book of Malachi, deals with the people's grudging giving to God (3:6–12); the other, the sixth and final disputation, addresses the problem of their arrogant accusations against God (3:13–4:3).

3:6–12 FIFTH DISPUTATION: GRUDGING GIVING TO GOD

The fifth disputation addresses the people's negligence in giving to the Lord. It begins by focusing on God's graciousness (3:6–7). Despite God's unchanging, unconditional love for them (3:6; see also 1:2), the people fail to honor and obey him (3:7; see also 1:6). One way in which they dishonor God is by failing to bring their tithes and offerings to him, thereby placing themselves under a curse (3:8–9). Malachi challenges the people to test God's faithfulness, assuring them that if they don't withhold their offerings and tithes, God will bless them abundantly (3:10–12).

3:6–7 A Gracious God

The section begins with an affirmation of God's graciousness to his people that is based on his unchanging character. The previous four disputations addressed the people's failures: they doubt his love (disputation 1), they fail to honor him (disputation 2), they are unfaithful in their covenant relationships (disputation 3), and they are unrighteous (disputation 4). Despite the disobedience and failures of his covenant people, God's covenant love is constant and he remains faithful to his covenant. He does not destroy his people but urges them, "Return to me, and I will return to you" (3:6–7). This is a call to repentance so that their relationship with the Lord may be restored and they may enjoy his blessing once more (see 1 Kgs 8:33–34).

3:8–9 The People's Failure to Give Generously

When the people inquire how they are to return to God, the Lord draws their attention to the matter of their grudging giving in response to his gracious love. Their repentance is to be expressed by generous and wholehearted offerings to

God. The charge that the people are "robbing" God is a serious accusation. It suggests that they are cheating the Lord by withholding what is due to him.

The Bible repeatedly affirms that the earth and everything in it belongs to God (Job 41:11; Ps 24:1); and yet, it pleases the Lord when his people respond to his generosity by their grateful and generous offerings. In the Torah, the tithe – which simply means a tenth – belongs to the Lord: "A tithe of everything from the land, whether grain from the soil or fruit from the trees, belongs to the LORD; it is holy to the LORD" (Lev 27:30). The people are to tithe the produce of the fields such as seed, grain, wine, oil, and the firstborn of their herds and flocks (Lev 27:30–33; Deut 14:22–23).

The practice of tithing began early in the patriarchal period, with Abram (Abraham) giving a tithe to Melchizedek, king of Salem (Gen 14:20; compare Heb 7:4–6). At Bethel, Jacob promised a tithe to God (Gen 28:18–22). Later, God commanded that tithes be given to sustain the Levites, who served in the tabernacle (Num 18:20–32), and to support needy groups such as foreigners, widows, and orphans (Deut 14:28–29).

An offering was a gift given to the Lord. In the Torah, offerings were given by the people for the construction of the tabernacle (Exod 25:2–8; 35:4–9). In later times, the people's gifts helped to maintain the temple (2 Kgs 12:9–16; 22:4–7). During the time of Nehemiah, the temple tax and the wood offerings were used for the upkeep of God's house (Neh 10:32–34).

God is the focus in all these tithes and offerings, which were expressions of love, honor, and gratitude. The people were able to give only because of God's abundant blessings (Deut 12:15); and the teaching on tithes and offerings emphasizes generous giving in response to these blessings. By failing to give their tithes and offerings, the people rob God of the respect due to him.

Contrary to what some Christians believe, tithing is not just an OT law that the NT abolishes. Although Jesus did not teach explicitly about tithing, he acknowledged the laws about tithing (Matt 23:23), assumed that his disciples would give generously (Matt 6:2–4), and praised a poor widow's sacrificial offering (Mark 12:41–44). Both the OT and the NT emphasize the principles of voluntary giving (Exod 35:5, 21–29; 2 Cor 8:12; 9:7), systematic giving in proportion to one's income (Deut 16:16–17; Acts 11:29; 1 Cor 16:1–2), responsibility and accountability in handling offerings (Neh 10:38–39; 13:12–13; 1 Cor 16:3–4), and giving that is both generous and ungrudging (Deut 15:10; 2 Cor 9:1–8). Echoing the OT language of sacrifices and offerings, Paul describes the Philippians' generous gift to him as "a fragrant offering, an acceptable sacrifice, pleasing to God" (Phil 4:18).

Offering back to God a portion of what he has graciously and generously placed in our hands reflects gratitude for his provision as well as love and respect for the giver of these good gifts. It is also one way in which we exercise responsible stewardship of the gifts God has entrusted to us. Just as in Malachi's time, the church needs leaders who will teach – by both word and example – the importance of this kind of giving.

The Asian economic crisis was a time of great trial for many. During this period, a certain Christian development company in the Philippines continued to practice the biblical principles of giving and generously supported God's work. Although most businesses in the Philippines and Asia were struggling financially, not only did this company's profits increase, they even won several awards for their performance. Their story became public when a Singaporean news station came to the Philippines to interview them.

Malachi warns of the consequences of robbing God (3:9). But he also assures the people that as they respond to God's love by generous giving, they will enjoy his abundant blessings (3:10–12).

3:10–12 God's Promise to Bless Abundantly

The command to bring "the whole tithe" into the storehouse is given because the people were "robbing" God of what was due him (3:8–9). The "whole tithe" represents wholehearted obedience. Tithes and offerings were necessary for the upkeep of the temple and its worship services (Neh 10:33) and to support those who served in God's house. During the postexilic era, many Levites deserted their duties in the temple and returned to the fields because there was no provision for their needs (Neh 13:10). In today's context, a congregation's tithes and offerings support pastors and church staff and help to maintain God's sanctuary and its ministries.

The people are invited to "test" God in this matter of tithing. As they give promptly, obediently, and wholeheartedly, God promises to "throw open the floodgates of heaven" and pour out abundant blessings (3:10). Plentiful rains translate into a bountiful harvest, negating the curse of disobedience (3:9).

While every farmer hopes for a good harvest, pests (literally, "eaters" or "devourers") destroy what the farmers have worked for. God, as the creator of every kind of living being, is sovereign over these devourers (Ps 68:30). His blessings include both protection from pests that devour the crops and unprecedented agricultural prosperity (3:11). These are some of the covenantal blessings promised to those who obey God.[1]

In the agricultural society of the postexilic era, the blessing of harvest is directly related to the people's crops and fields. Although this teaching may not apply directly to most of us, the underlying principles still hold true. Whether in the home or the workplace, the school or the marketplace, God protects and blesses the work of our hands according to his will. We can trust in his wisdom, protection, and love.

As God blesses the land, it becomes "a delightful land," causing "all the nations" to notice and affirm that the people of God are "blessed" (3:12; compare Zeph 3:19–20). Such pronouncements are beatitudes, affirming what God has done for his people and bringing glory and honor to God among the nations.

3:13–4:3 SIXTH DISPUTATION: ARROGANT ACCUSATIONS AGAINST GOD

The sixth disputation focuses on the people's arrogant accusations against God (3:13–4:3). The people allege that it is futile to serve God because he does not reward the righteous and punish evildoers (3:13–15). God responds to these allegations by assuring his people that those who fear him and honor him will enjoy his blessings while those who persist in evil will be judged (3:16–4:3).

Malachi divides the people into two groups. First, there are those who revere, obey, and serve the Lord (3:16–18; 4:2). Second, there are those who are arrogant, evildoers, and wicked (3:13, 18; 4:1, 3).

3:13–15 The People's Allegations against God

This disputation addresses a serious problem. It appears that those who serve God are complaining that they gain nothing by serving God (3:14), while those who do evil are prospering (3:15). Their words are bitter, and they act like mourners who grieve over God's injustice.

In the fourth disputation, the people "wearied" God by claiming that "all who do evil are good in the eyes of the LORD, and he is pleased with them" and by questioning God's justice (2:17). Now they make the even more serious claim that "it is futile to serve God" (3:14a). Their words show that they are not serving God out of love or respect but only for what they can expect to gain. That is why the Lord charges, "You have spoken arrogantly against me" (3:13).

---

1. See Deuteronomy 28:1–13.

As before, the people fail to recognize their own shortcomings. They are confident that they are "carrying out his requirements" – a reference to obedience to God (3:14a; see Gen 26:5; Deut 11:1). The reference to "going about like mourners" refers to their gestures of penitence and repentance (3:14b; Ps 38:4–6). But complying with commandments or carrying out mourning rituals without a genuine desire to honor God is not acceptable service in God's eyes.

The Lord "listened" to his people's conversations and "heard" their heart cries (3:16). It is not only by answering prayers that God expresses his care for his people but also by being attentive to them and taking seriously their concerns and frustrations.

3:16–4:3 God Answers His People

In this section (3:16–4:3), the prophet shifts his focus to those who "feared the LORD" (3:16), were his "treasured possession" (3:17), and revered his name (4:1). He begins by talking about those who fear God. These are probably not a different group from those who had spoken arrogantly against the Lord (3:13–15) but, rather, those who have taken to heart God's rebuke, discussed the matter among themselves, and now seek to honor God's name (3:16).

The OT has three types of precious records: first, the book of life, which records the names of those who are in a righteous relationship with the Lord (Exod 32:32); second, the registry of people that records their birthplaces (Ps 87:4–6); and third, the scroll of remembrance, a historical record similar to Chronicles (3:16b). In the postexilic era, the names of returnees and their ancestors were recorded as a remembrance (1 Chr 1–9; Ezra 2; Neh 7) and the names of those who served as priests and Levites were also recorded by Nehemiah (Neh 12:1–26). During the Persian era, the royal archives recorded important events and the names of those who had rendered valuable services to the king (Esth 6:1–2). In Malachi, the "scroll of remembrance" records the names of "those who feared the LORD and honored his name" (3:16b; see also Exod 32:32; Isa 4:3; Phil 4:3; Rev 3:5; 20:12).

Asian cultures are primarily oral cultures, with family histories and the Christian faith often being passed on orally. But this does not mean that written records are unimportant, for these may preserve the precious stories of our faith and spur on future generations to faithfulness.

With God, to remember is to act (Gen 8:1; Exod 2:24–25). As God remembers those who fear him, he will act on their behalf. These people belong to him and enjoy the privileged status of being his "treasured possession" (3:17; Exod 19:5). The OT portrays the Israelites as God's treasure in two ways: first, their unchangeable status as God's "inheritance" (Deut 4:20); second, their individual status of being in relationship with God (Exod 19:5). This latter privileged status of being God's treasured possession requires holy living (Deut 7:6; 14:2; 26:18–19). In the NT, too, God's people are described as God's "special possession" and called to be a "holy nation" (1 Pet 2:9).

God refers to Israel as his firstborn son (Exod 4:22; Jer 31:9). Malachi uses this father-son imagery to depict the close and affectionate relationship between God and his people (3:17b; compare Ps 103:13; Hos 11:1). The Lord punished the firstborn of the Egyptians but spared the firstborn of the Israelites (Exod 12:26–29). On the day of judgment, God will spare those who fear him and honor his name (3:17–18).

"On the day when I act" (3:17) is a reference to the day of the Lord – and this "day that is coming" (4:1) is the day of judgment. On this day, the "distinction between the righteous and the wicked" will be evident to all. The righteous are those who serve God because they seek to honor his name (3:16); the wicked are those who do not serve God and, instead, speak arrogantly against him (3:13) and are self-seeking, looking only to their own "gain" (3:14).

For the arrogant and the evildoers, the day of the Lord will be a day of fearful punishment (4:1). Earlier, Malachi used the image of a refining fire (3:2); now he speaks of a destructive fire which will swiftly and surely destroy everything (4:1). In the OT, burning stubble symbolized divine punishment (Joel 2:5; Obad 18; Nah 1:10). God's judgment will also be thorough – "not a root or a branch" will be spared (4:1b) and only "ashes" will remain (4:3). On that day, evildoers will be utterly destroyed! This answers the people's question about why God lets evildoers prosper (3:15). Although such people may prosper for a while, ultimately, they will face God's wrath.

But for those who revere God, the day of the Lord holds out the promise of great reward. The "sun of righteousness will rise," not with the unbearable heat of judgment but with a blessing of "healing" like that promised in Isaiah 30:26. This will cause the righteous to rejoice, like well-fed calves enjoying a carefree frolic (4:2). God has not forgotten either the wicked or the righteous; his judgment and his vindication simply await the opportune time.

MALACHI 4:4–6

CONCLUSION: REMINDER

FROM THE LORD

The prophet Malachi is indeed the messenger of God to his people in their hour of need. These closing verses form a fitting conclusion not only to the book of Malachi but also to the "Book of the Twelve" – that is, the Minor Prophets. Malachi, and thus the OT, ends with God's promise of a messenger who is to come (4:5; see also 3:1–4) and the NT begins with the coming of John the Baptist, God's messenger who comes in the spirit of Elijah to prepare the way for the Lord (Luke 1:16–17; 3:1–8).

The book of Malachi ends with a reminder, a promise, and a warning. First, the people are reminded to uphold the covenant, entered into at Horeb (Sinai), which formed the basis of God's relationship with his people (4:4). But to "remember" also entails action. Hence this is a call to repentance and return to the Lord through obedience to the Mosaic law (4:4). This book that has emphasized the importance of God's messenger (2:7; 3:1) now concludes with a reference to Moses, that great messenger and servant of God who was commissioned to instruct God's people in his law:[1] "Remember the law of my servant Moses, the decrees and laws I gave him at Horeb for all Israel" (4:4).

Second, God promises to send another messenger, a prophet who will turn the hearts of the people back to God (4:5–6). This messenger is identified as "the prophet Elijah." The Jews regarded Elijah as a second Moses. Just as Moses spent forty nights and forty days at Mount Horeb (Exod 24:18), Elijah spent forty nights and forty days traveling to Mount Horeb (1 Kgs 19:8). Elijah's message was one of reconciliation and restoration of relationships – both with God and within the community of God's people. The NT interprets the promised Elijah as John the Baptist (Matt 11:7–15). Another messenger, the angel of the Lord, confirms that John's ministry will fulfill Malachi's prophecy: "He will bring back many of the people of Israel to the Lord their God. And he will go on before the Lord, in the spirit and power of Elijah, to turn the

---

1. See Exodus 19.

hearts of the parents to their children and the disobedient to the wisdom of the righteous – to make ready a people prepared for the Lord" (Luke 1:16–17).

Third, Malachi repeats his warning about the coming day of the Lord (4:5; see also 3:2; 4:1; Joel 2:31). This "great and dreadful day" will bring "total destruction" to those who refuse to repent and return to the Lord. Malachi has already stressed the importance of turning or returning to the Lord. The proper teaching of the priests will turn sinners from their sins (2:6). The people are to return to God so that God may return to them (3:7). And now, the coming prophet will "turn the hearts of the parents to their children, and the hearts of the children to their parents" (4:6).

Although Malachi presents six disputations, the book ends on a note of hope. God will send his messenger and turn the people's hearts towards him. They will understand that he loves them and deals with them in justice and mercy. They, in turn, should continue to remember the law of his servant Moses and obey its decrees before the coming of the day of the Lord. The hope of Malachi has been realized, first, in the coming of John the Baptist, and fully and finally, in the one for whom John prepared the way – the Lord Jesus Christ. In him, we understand the love and justice of the Lord.

SELECTED BIBLIOGRAPHY

Ademiluka, Solomon S. "A Study of Malachi 3:8–12 in Relation to Tithing in Some Churches in Nigeria." *OTE* 33 (2020): 285–305.

———. "'For I Hate Divorce,' Says the Lord: Interpreting Malachi 2:16 in Relation to Prohibition of Divorce in Some Churches in Nigeria." *OTE* 32 (2019): 846–868.

Armerding, Carl E. "Nahum." In EBC, Revised, Vol. 8. Grand Rapids: Zondervan, 2008.

Assis, Elie. *The Book of Joel: A Prophet between Calamity and Hope.* New York: Bloomsbury, 2013.

———. "Moses, Elijah and the Messianic Hope: A New Reading of Malachi 3, 22–24." *ZAW* 123 (2011): 207–220.

———. "The Date and Meaning of the Book of Joel." *VT* 61 (2011): 163–183.

Baker, David W. *Joel, Obadiah, Malachi.* NIVAC Old Testament. Grand Rapids: Zondervan, 2006.

Bang, Seung Ho. "For Whom the Plowshares and Pruning Toil: A Tradition-Historical Reading of Joel 4.10." *JSOT* 39.4 (2015): 489–512.

Barton, John. *Joel and Obadiah.* OTL. Louisville: Westminster John Knox Press, 2001.

Berlinger, Joshua, Julia Hollingsworth, Zamira Rahim, and Adam Renton. "Coronavirus Pandemic: Updates from Around the World." Online: https://www.cnn.com/world/live-news/coronavirus-pandemic-05-11-20-intl/index.html.

Boloje, Blessing Onoriode. "Returning to Yahweh and Yahweh's Return: Aspects of שוב in the Book of Malachi." *OTE* 33 (2020): 143–161.

Brown, William P. *Obadiah Through Malachi.* WeBC. Louisville: Westminster John Knox, 1996.

Bruckner, James. *Jonah, Nahum, Habakkuk, Zephaniah.* NIVAC Old Testament. Grand Rapids: Zondervan, 2004.

Burnside, Jonathan. *God, Justice, and Society: Aspects of Law and Legality in the Bible.* Oxford: Oxford University Press, 2011.

Butterworth, G. M. "Nahum." In NBC, 21st Century Edition. 4th ed. Edited by D. A. Carson et al. Leicester: Inter-Varsity Press, 1994.

Carlson, Darren. "When Muslims Dream of Jesus." Online: https://www.thegospelcoalition.org/article/muslims-dream-jesus/.

Casayuran, Mario B. "3 'Sex-For-Fly' Victims Get Assistance." Manila Bulletin, Vol. 486, no. 27 (June 27, 2013): 6.

Chan, Patrick Yi-Sang. "Romans 8 and the Chinese Concept of Shame and Guilt." In *Missio Dei: A Journal of Missional Theology and Praxis* 1 (2020). Online: http://missiodeijournal.com/issues/md-11/authors/md-11-chan.

Chapman, Gary. *The 5 Love Languages: The Secret to Love That Lasts*. Reprint. Chicago: Northfield Publishing, 2015.

Cheung, Luke L., and Andrew Spurgeon. *James: A Pastoral and Contextual Commentary*. ABCS. Carlisle: Langham Global Library, 2018.

Christensen, Duane L. *Nahum: A New Translation with Introduction and Commentary*. AYBC. New Haven: Yale University Press, 2009.

Coggins, Richard. "Joel." *CBR* 2 (2003): 85–103.

Cook, Gregory. "Nahum Prophetic Name." *TynBul* 67 (2016): 37–40.

———. "Nahum's Shaking Cypresses." *BBR* 26 (2016): 1–6.

Cook, Gregory D. "Of Gods and Kings: Ashur Imagery in Nahum." *BBR* 29 (2019): 19–31.

Crenshaw, James L. *Joel: A New Translation with Introduction and Commentary*. AYBC. New Haven: Yale University Press, 1995.

Dillard, Raymond B., and Tremper Longman III. *An Introduction to the Old Testament*. Grand Rapids: Zondervan, 1994.

Finley, Thomas J. *Joel, Amos, Obadiah*. WEC. Chicago: Moody Press, 1996.

Gibson, Jonathan. "Covenant Continuity and Fidelity in Malachi." *TynBul* 66 (2015): 313–316.

———. "Cutting Off 'Kith and Kin,' 'Er and Onan'? Interpreting an Obscure Phrase in Mal 2:12." *JBL* 133 (2014): 519–537.

Golani, Shira J. "Swords That Are Ploughshares: Another Case of (Bilingual) Wordplay in Biblical Prophecy." *Biblica* 98 (2017): 425–434.

Goldingay, John. *Old Testament Theology. Volume 1: Israel's Gospel*. Downers Grove: IVP Academic, 2003.

———. *Old Testament Theology. Volume 2: Israel's Faith*. Downers Grove: IVP Academic, 2006.

———. *Old Testament Theology. Volume 3: Israel's Life*. Downers Grove: IVP Academic, 2009.

Goldingay, John, and Pamela J. Sealise. *Minor Prophets II*. NIBC. Peabody: Hendrickson, 2009.

Gowan, Donald E. *Theology of the Prophetic Books: The Death & Resurrection of Israel*. Louisville: Westminster John Knox, 1998.

Hawker, Luke. "Locust Invasion Warning: China on the Brink of 'Disaster' – Officials on Alert." Online: https://www.express.co.uk/news/world/1307920/locust-swarm-invasion-china-news-latest-locust-plague-laos.

Herion, Gary A. "Wrath of God." In AYBD, Vol. 6. Edited by David Noel Freedman et al. New York: Doubleday, 1992.

Hill, Andrew E. *Malachi. A New Translation with Introduction and Commentary*. AYBC. New York: Doubleday, 1998.

Hubbard, David A. *Joel and Amos: An Introduction and Commentary*. TOTC. Downers Grove: InterVarsity Press, 1989.

Hwang, Jerry. "How Long Will My Glory Be Reproach?: Honour and Shame in Old Testament Lament Traditions." *OTE* 30 (2017): 684–706.

Joseph, Joel. "Joel." In *SABC*. Carlisle: Langham, 2015.

Kaiser, Walter C. Jr. *Malachi: God's Unchanging Love*. Grand Rapids: Baker, 1984.

Kang, Bin. "The Positive Value of Shame for Post-Exilic Returnees in Ezra/Nehemiah." *OTE* 33 (2020): 250–265.

Kötenberger, Andreas J., and David A. Croteau. "'Will a Man Rob God?' (Malachi 3:8): A Study of Tithing in the Old and New Testaments." *BBR* 16 (2006): 53–77.

Krause, Joachim J. "Tradition, History and Our Story: Some Observation on Jacob and Esau in the Books of Obadiah and Malachi." *JSOT* 32 (2008): 477–486.

Lewis, C. S. *The Problem of Pain*. OCR, 1940; New York: Macmillan, 1947; Reprinted, Quebec: Samizdat University Press, 2016.

Li, Jin, Lianqin Wang, and Kurt W. Fisher. "The Organization of Chinese Shame Concepts." *Cognition and Emotion* 18 (2004): 767–797.

Limburg, James. *Hosea–Micah. Interpretation: A Bible Commentary for Teaching and Preaching*. Atlanta: John Knox, 1988.

Malone, Andrew S. "Is the Messiah Announced in Malachi 3:1?" *TynBul* 57 (2006): 216–228.

Mariottini, Claude F. "Malachi the Prophet of His Time." *JBQ* 1998 (26): 149–157.

Mark, Joshua J. "Assyrian Warfare." Online: https://www.ancient.eu/Assyrian_Warfare/.

Merrill, Eugene H. *An Exegetical Commentary: Haggai, Zechariah, Malachi*. Chicago: Moody, 1994. Reprint. Dallas: Biblical Studies Press, 2003.

Miller, Patrick D. *The Way of the Lord: Essays on Old Testament Theology*. Grand Rapids: Eerdmans, 2004.

Miller, Rebecca Florence. "When Does the Bible Allow Divorce?" *Christianity Today*, April, 2016. Online: https://www.christianitytoday.com/ct/2016/april-web-only/when-does-bible-allow-divorce.html.

O'Brien, Julia M. *Challenging Prophetic Metaphor: Theology and Ideology in the Prophets*. Louisville: Westminster John Knox Press, 2008.

———. *Nahum*. London: Sheffield Academic Press, 2002.

———. "Nahum–Habakkuk–Zephaniah: Reading the 'Former Prophets' in the Persian Period." *Int* 61 (2007): 168–183.

O'Hara-Glaspie, Kristy J. "Prayers for People Affected by the New Coronavirus." Online: https://www.worldvision.org/disaster-relief-news-stories/prayers-people-affected-new-coronavirus.

Patterson, Richard D. "Joel." In EBC, Revised, Vol. 8. Grand Rapids: Zondervan, 2008.

———. *Nahum, Habakkuk, Zephaniah*. WEC. Chicago: Moody, 1991.

Petersen, David I. *Zechariah 9–14 and Malachi*. OTL. Louisville: Westminster, 1995.

Pinker, Aron. "Descent of the Goddess Ishtar to the Netherworld and Nahum II 8." *VT* 55 (2005): 89–100.

———. "Nineveh's Defensive Strategy and Nahum 2–3." *ZAW* 118 (2006): 618–625.

———. "On the Meaning of *htkbd* in Nahum III:15." *VT* 53 (2003): 558–561.

Ramachandra, Vinoth. *Sarah's Laughter: Doubt, Tears, and Christian Hope*. Carlisle: Langham Global Library, 2020.

Raquiza, Marivic. "Couplings and Un–Couplings in a Land without Divorce." Online: https://www. International-divorce.com/d-philippines.

Redditt, P. L. *Haggai, Zechariah, Malachi*. NCBC. Grand Rapids: Eerdmans, 1995.

Schart, Aaron. "The First Section of the Book of the Twelve Prophets: Hosea-Joel Amos." *Int* 61 (2007): 138–152.

Shao, Joseph T. "Spirituality in the Prophetic Traditions: An Asian Perspective." In *Perjuangan Menatang Zaman (Kumpulan esai sebagai penghargaan kepada Pendeta Stephen Tong, pada HUT ke–60, Festschrift for Stephen Tong)*. Edited by Hendra G. Mulia. Jakarta: Reformed Institute Press, 2000.

Shao, Joseph Too, and Rosa Ching Shao. *Ezra and Nehemiah: A Pastoral and Contextual Commentary*. ABCS. Carlisle: Langham Global Library, 2019.

Shao, Rosa C. *Chinese-Filipino Adolescents' Developing Autonomy in the Context of Parent-Adolescent Conflict and Family Cohesion*. PhD Dissertation. Quezon City: Ateneo de Manila University, 2006.

———. "Anger Management or Mismanagement: When It Thunders It Roars or Rolls!" In *Expanding Horizons: Theological Reflections*. Edited by Joseph T. Shao, Rosa C. Shao, and Jean U. Uayan. Valenzuela City: Biblical Seminary of the Philippines, 2010.

———. *Jonah: A Pastoral and Contextual Commentary*. ABCS. Carlisle: Langham Global Library, 2019.

———. "The Role of the Church under Climate Change." *Evangelical Today* 40 (2014): 20–21.

Simkins, Ronald A. "'Return to Yahweh': Honor and Shame in Joel." *Semeia* 68 (1994): 41–54.

Stokes, Ryan E. "I, Yhwh, Have Not Changed? Reconsidering the Translation of Malachi 3:6; Lamentations 4:1; and Proverbs 24:21–22." *CBQ* 70 (2008): 264–276.

Stone, Madeline. "A Plague of Locust Has Descended on East Africa. Climate Change May Be to Blame." Online: https://www.nationalgeographic.com/science/2020/02/locust-plague-climate-science-east-africa/.

Stuart, Douglas. *Hosea–Jonah*. WBC. Waco: Word, 1987.

———. "Malachi." In *The Minor Prophets: An Exegetical and Expository Commentary*. Volume 3. Edited by Thomas McComisky. Grand Rapids: Baker, 1998.

Tira, Sadiri Joy, and Juliet Uytanlet. *A Hybrid World: Diaspora, Hybridity, and Missio Dei*. Littleton: William Carey Publishing, 2020.

Uytanlet, Samson L. "The Sound of Silence: A Literary Comparison between Jose Rizal's *Noli Me Tangere* and John of Patmos' *Revelation of Jesus*." In *Scripture and Service: A Celebration of Life, Essays in Honor of Joseph Shao*. Edited by Samson L. Uytanlet. Valenzuela City: Biblical Seminary of the Philippines, 2019.

Uytanlet, Samson, with Kiem-Kiok Kwa. *Matthew: A Pastoral and Contextual Commentary*. ABCS. Carlisle: Langham Global Library, 2017.

Verhoef, Peter A. *Haggai and Malachi*. NICOT. Grand Rapids: Eerdmans, 1987.

Weiten, Wayne. *Psychology: Themes & Variations. 6th ed.* New York: Wadsworth/Thomson Learning, 2004.

Wood, Julie. "West as Nineveh: How Does Nahum's Message of Judgment Apply to Today." *Themelios* 31 (2005): 7–37.

Wright, J. S. "Day of the Lord." In NBD, 3rd edition. Edited by D. R. W. Wood. Leicester: Inter-Varsity Press, 1996.

Zehnder, Markus, "A Fresh Look at Malachi II 13–16." *VT* 53 (2003): 224–259.

Asia Theological Association
54 Scout Madriñan St. Quezon City 1103, Philippines
Email: ataasia@gmail.com Telefax: (632) 410 0312

OUR MISSION

The Asia Theological Association (ATA) is a body of theological institutions, committed to evangelical faith and scholarship, networking together to serve the Church in equipping the people of God for the mission of the Lord Jesus Christ.

OUR COMMITMENT

The ATA is committed to serving its members in the development of evangelical, biblical theology by strengthening interaction, enhancing scholarship, promoting academic excellence, fostering spiritual and ministerial formation and mobilizing resources to fulfill God's global mission within diverse Asian cultures.

OUR TASK

Affirming our mission and commitment, ATA seeks to:

- **Strengthen** interaction through inter-institutional fellowship and programs, regional and continental activities, faculty and student exchange programs.
- **Enhance** scholarship through consultations, workshops, seminars, publications, and research fellowships.
- **Promote** academic excellence through accreditation standards, faculty and curriculum development.
- **Foster** spiritual and ministerial formation by providing mentor models, encouraging the development of ministerial skills and a Christian ethos.
- **Mobilize** resources through library development, information technology and infra-structural development.

To learn more about ATA, visit www.ataasia.com or facebook.com/AsiaTheologicalAssociation

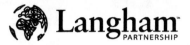

Langham Literature, along with its publishing work, is a ministry of Langham Partnership.

Langham Partnership is a global fellowship working in pursuit of the vision God entrusted to its founder John Stott –

> *to facilitate the growth of the church in maturity and Christ-likeness through raising the standards of biblical preaching and teaching.*

Our vision is to see churches in the Majority World equipped for mission and growing to maturity in Christ through the ministry of pastors and leaders who believe, teach and live by the word of God.

Our mission is to strengthen the ministry of the word of God through:
- nurturing national movements for biblical preaching
- fostering the creation and distribution of evangelical literature
- enhancing evangelical theological education

especially in countries where churches are under-resourced.

Our ministry

Langham Preaching partners with national leaders to nurture indigenous biblical preaching movements for pastors and lay preachers all around the world. With the support of a team of trainers from many countries, a multi-level programme of seminars provides practical training, and is followed by a programme for training local facilitators. Local preachers' groups and national and regional networks ensure continuity and ongoing development, seeking to build vigorous movements committed to Bible exposition.

Langham Literature provides Majority World preachers, scholars and seminary libraries with evangelical books and electronic resources through publishing and distribution, grants and discounts. The programme also fosters the creation of indigenous evangelical books in many languages, through writer's grants, strengthening local evangelical publishing houses, and investment in major regional literature projects, such as one volume Bible commentaries like the *Africa Bible Commentary* and the *South Asia Bible Commentary*.

Langham Scholars provides financial support for evangelical doctoral students from the Majority World so that, when they return home, they may train pastors and other Christian leaders with sound, biblical and theological teaching. This programme equips those who equip others. Langham Scholars also works in partnership with Majority World seminaries in strengthening evangelical theological education. A growing number of Langham Scholars study in high quality doctoral programmes in the Majority World itself. As well as teaching the next generation of pastors, graduated Langham Scholars exercise significant influence through their writing and leadership.

To learn more about Langham Partnership and the work we do visit **langham.org**

CPSIA information can be obtained
at www.ICGtesting.com
Printed in the USA
FSHW020759140721